Echoes of Insight: A Collector's Journey

by Douglas Murray

Contents

Preface

Within the boundless realm of literature, there exists a profound treasure trove of human wisdom, encapsulated in the form of aphorisms, maxims, quotes, and reflections. These concise expressions of profound thought have the power to transcend time, culture, and language, resonating with readers across generations. It is within this realm that our tale begins—a tale of a passionate and dedicated collector, Douglas Murray, who embarks on an extraordinary quest to compile the essence of human wisdom found within the pages of countless books.

Douglas Murray, a lifelong lover of literature, found himself inexorably drawn to the power and beauty of concise yet profound insights scattered throughout the written word. It was his insatiable curiosity and deep appreciation for the human intellect that led him to embark on a remarkable journey—to explore the vast expanse of human knowledge and distill its essence into a singular collection.

With unwavering determination and an unquenchable thirst for knowledge, Douglas Murray traversed the hallowed halls of libraries, delving into the ancient tomes of philosophers, the timeless works of poets, and the contemplative musings of scholars. He sought out the rare and forgotten volumes, lost in the annals of history, and meticulously transcribed the aphorisms, maxims, quotes, and reflections that resonated with his soul.

As Douglas immersed himself in the pursuit of wisdom, he realized that each book he encountered was a portal into the minds of its creators. The collection he curated became a testament to the collective knowledge, experiences, and aspirations of humanity. It transcended the boundaries of time and geography, weaving together the threads of wisdom from ancient civilizations, medieval scholars, Renaissance thinkers, and modern luminaries.

Through his tireless efforts, Douglas Murray gradually pieced together a vast mosaic of human intellect. His collection became a reflection of the human condition, capturing the breadth and depth of human emotions, struggles, triumphs, and dreams. Each entry within his repository of wisdom served as a window into the multifaceted nature of existence, a catalyst for introspection, and a source of inspiration for those who sought meaning and understanding.

In this book, Echoes of Insight: A Collector's Journey we invite you to embark on a remarkable journey alongside Douglas Murray. Through the pages that follow, you will explore the vast tapestry of human thought, woven together by the delicate threads of aphorisms, maxims, quotes, and reflections. As you immerse yourself in the richness of these distilled insights, may you find illumination, solace, and a renewed appreciation for the collective wisdom of humanity.

Remember, dear reader, wisdom is not confined to a single source or era; it is a timeless and boundless treasure that awaits discovery by those who possess the audacity to seek it. So, join us as we venture into the uncharted territories of the human intellect, guided by the extraordinary journey of Douglas Murray and his relentless pursuit of wisdom.

François de la Rochefoucauld

1. What we term virtue is often but a mass of various actions and divers interests, which fortune, or our own industry, manage to arrange; and it is not always from valor or from chastity that men are brave, and women chaste.

2. Self-love is the greatest of flatterers.

3. Whatever discoveries have been made in the region of self-love, there remain many unexplored territories there.

4. Self-love is more cunning than the most cunning man in the world.

5. The duration of our passions is no more dependant upon us than the duration of our life.

6. Passion often renders the most clever man a fool, and even sometimes renders the most foolish man clever.

7. Great and striking actions which dazzle the eyes are represented by politicians as the effect of great designs, instead of which they are commonly caused by the temper and the passions. Thus the war between Augustus and Anthony, which is set down to the ambition they entertained of making themselves masters of the world, was probably but an effect of jealousy.

8. The passions are the only advocates which always persuade. They are a natural art, the rules of which are infallible; and the simplest man with passion will be more persuasive than the most eloquent without.

9. The passions possess a certain injustice and self-interest which makes it dangerous to follow them, and in reality we should distrust them even when they appear most trustworthy.

10. In the human heart there is a perpetual generation of passions; so that the ruin of one is almost always the foundation of another.

11. Passions often produce their contraries: avarice sometimes leads to prodigality, and prodigality to avarice; we are often obstinate through weakness and daring though timidity.

12.   Whatever care we take to conceal our passions under the appearances of piety and honour, they are always to be seen through these veils.

13. Our self-love endures more impatiently the condemnation of our tastes than of our opinions.

14. Men are not only prone to forget benefits and injuries; they even hate those who have obliged them, and cease to hate those who have injured them. The necessity of revenging an injury or of recompensing a benefit seems a slavery to which they are unwilling to submit.

15. The affections of the people are often won by the clemency of Princes, which is frequently a policy employed.

16. Often, the clemency that they claim as merit arises from vanity, idleness, fear, or a combination of all three.

17. The moderation of those who are happy is a result of the calm bestowed upon their temperament by good fortune.

18. Moderation is driven by the fear of arousing envy and contempt, qualities associated with those intoxicated by their good fortune. It is a vain exhibition of strength of mind, and in essence, the moderation displayed by individuals at the pinnacle of success is merely a desire to appear greater than their circumstances.

19. We all possess sufficient strength to endure the misfortunes suffered by others.

20. The constancy exhibited by the wise is merely their talent for concealing the inner turmoil of their hearts.

21. At times, those condemned to death feign constancy and contempt for their impending fate, which is in reality a fear of confronting it. Thus, this constancy and contempt serve as a blindfold for their minds, much like a bandage over their eyes.

22.   Philosophy easily triumphs over past and future evils, but present afflictions often triumph over philosophy itself.

23. Few individuals truly understand death; instead, we endure it out of determination, stupidity, and habit. Most people perish because they do not know how to prevent their own demise.

24. When great men allow themselves to be overwhelmed by persistent misfortune, it reveals that their resilience was sustained solely by ambition, not their intellect. Thus, in addition to immense vanity, heroes are made just like ordinary men.

25. Greater virtues are required to withstand good fortune than misfortune.

26. Neither the sun nor death can be stared at without blinking.

27. People often take pride in their passions, even the worst ones, but envy is a timid and bashful passion that no one dares openly confess.

28. Jealousy, in a sense, is just and reasonable as it strives to safeguard a good that belongs to us or that we believe belongs to us. On the other hand, envy is a furious emotion that cannot tolerate the happiness of others.

29. The evil deeds we commit do not attract as much persecution and hatred as our good qualities do.

30. We possess more strength than willpower, and often we declare things as impossible merely as an excuse.

31. If we were devoid of faults, we would not derive such pleasure from observing the faults of others.

32. Jealousy thrives on doubt and transforms into fury as soon as doubt transforms into certainty.

33. Pride indemnifies itself and suffers no loss, even when it discards vanity.

34. If we lacked pride, we would not complain about the pride of others.

35. Pride is essentially the same in all individuals; the only variation lies in the manner and method in which it is displayed.

36. It seems that nature, which has wisely organized the organs of our body for our happiness, has also bestowed upon us pride to shield us from the humiliation of acknowledging our imperfections.

37. Pride plays a more significant role than goodness in our reprimands of those who commit faults. We reproach them not so much to correct them, but to persuade them that we ourselves are free from faults.

38. We make promises based on our hopes and fulfill them based on our fears.

39. Interest speaks in various tongues and assumes different roles, including that of disinterestedness.

40. Interest blinds some individuals and enables others to see.

41. Those who immerse themselves excessively in trivial matters often become incapable of accomplishing great things.

43. Our reason exceeds our strength; we are unable to follow all the guidance it offers.

42. A man often believes himself to be a leader when, in fact, he is being led astray. While his mind endeavors to pursue one goal, his heart unwittingly pulls him toward another.

44. The terms strength and weakness of the mind are misnomers; they are merely reflections of the favorable or unfavorable arrangement of our bodily organs.

45. The capriciousness of our temperament is even more unpredictable than that of Fortune.

46. The attachment or indifference exhibited by philosophers toward life is merely a manifestation of their self-love. It is a quality no more debatable than that of the palate or one's preference for certain colors.

47. Our temperament places a value on every gift bestowed upon us by fortune.

48. Happiness resides in personal preferences and not in the objects themselves. We derive joy from possessing what we love, not what others love.

49. We are never as happy or as unhappy as we imagine ourselves to be.

50. Those who believe they possess merit convince themselves that they are honored by their unhappiness, in an attempt to persuade both others and themselves that they are deserving of Fortune's whims.

51. Nothing should diminish our self-satisfaction more than observing that we disapprove today of what we approved of yesterday.

52. Regardless of the disparities in our fortunes, there exists a certain balance of good and evil that renders them equal.

53. No matter the natural advantages one possesses, it is not nature alone but also fortune that shapes a hero.

54. The philosophers' disdain for wealth merely conceals their desire for vengeance against the injustice of fortune, by scorning the very goods that fortune has deprived them of. It is a secret means of protecting themselves against the degradation of poverty and a roundabout path to achieving the distinction that riches could not provide.

55. The hatred of favorites is simply a love for favoritism. The envy of not possessing favor consoles and alleviates its regrets through the contempt it displays for those who possess it. Thus, we withhold our admiration from them, unable to detract from what captures the rest of the world's attention.

56. To establish ourselves in the world, we go to great lengths to appear as if we are already established.

57. Although men boast about their grand actions, they are not often the result of a grand design but rather chance occurrences.

58. It appears that our actions have auspicious or inauspicious stars to which we attribute a great portion of the praise or blame bestowed upon them.

59. There are no accidents so unfortunate that skillful individuals cannot derive some advantage from them, nor are there any fortunate events that foolish individuals cannot turn to their own detriment.

60. Fortune bends all things to the advantage of those whom she favors.

61. The happiness or unhappiness of individuals depends not only on their circumstances but also on their dispositions.

62. Sincerity is an expression of an open heart, but it is a quality found in very few people. What we typically witness is artful dissimulation aimed at gaining the trust of others.

63. Our aversion to lying often masks an ambition to make our words credible and weighty, lending a sense of solemnity to our conversations.

64. Truth does not yield as much good in the world as its counterfeits do evil.

65. Praise for prudence knows no bounds, yet it cannot guarantee even the smallest outcome.

66. A clever individual should arrange their interests in a manner that allows each one to be pursued in due order. Our greed often troubles us, compelling us to chase after numerous things simultaneously, resulting in an eagerness for the insignificant while missing out on the truly significant.

67. Good sense is to the mind what grace is to the body. 68. Defining love is a difficult task. All we can say is that, in the soul, it is a desire for dominance; in the mind, it is a sympathy; and in the body, it is a hidden and delicate wish to possess what we love—accompanied by many mysteries.

69. If pure love exists, free from the mixture of our other passions, it resides concealed deep within the heart, even unknown to ourselves.

70. Where love exists, no disguise can conceal it for long; where it does not, no pretense can fabricate it.

71. There are few people who would not feel ashamed of being beloved when they no longer love.

72. If we judge love by its most common outcomes, it more closely resembles hatred than friendship.

73. We may encounter women who have never engaged in an affair, but it is rare to find those who have engaged in only one.

74. There is only one type of love, but there are countless variations.

75. Neither love nor fire can persist without perpetual motion. Both cease to exist as soon as hope or fear fades away.

76. True love is as elusive as real ghosts; it is a topic much discussed but experienced by few.

77. Love is often associated with various transactions and enterprises that are falsely attributed to it. However, love is not concerned with these matters any more than the Doge is with all that transpires in Venice.

78. The love of justice, for most individuals, is simply a fear of experiencing injustice.

79. Silence is the wisest choice for those who lack self-confidence.

80. The reason for our fickleness in friendship lies in the difficulty of knowing the qualities of the soul, while the qualities of the mind are easily discernible.

81. We can only love that which is in harmony with ourselves, and we can truly prioritize our friends over ourselves when we prefer our friends based on our taste or pleasure. It is through this preference that friendship becomes genuine and perfect.

82. Reconciliation with our enemies is merely a desire to improve our own situation, a weariness of conflict, and a fear of unfortunate consequences.

83. What people often label as friendship is nothing more than a partnership based on mutual interests and the exchange of favors. In truth, it is a trade in which self-love always expects to gain something.

84. It is more disgraceful to distrust others than to be deceived by our friends.

85. We often convince ourselves to love those more powerful than us, yet it is self-interest alone that drives our friendship. We do not give away our hearts for the good we wish to do but for the benefits we expect to receive.

86. Our distrust of others justifies their deceit.

87. Men would not long survive in society if they were not duped by one another.

88. Self-love enhances or diminishes the good qualities of our friends based on the satisfaction we derive from them. We judge their merit by their actions toward us.

89. Everyone criticizes their memory, but no one criticizes their judgment.

90. In the course of social interaction, we please others more with our faults than with our virtues.

91. The loftiest ambition appears the least ambitious when faced with insurmountable obstacles to achieving its goal.

92. To awaken a person deluded about their own merit is as detrimental to them as it was to the Athenian madman who delighted in believing that all the ships docking in the harbor belonged to him.

93. Old men take pleasure in offering good advice as a consolation for no longer being able to set bad examples.

94. Great names degrade rather than elevate those who do not know how to live up to them.

95. The mark of extraordinary merit is to witness those who envy it most despise it least.

96. Perhaps a man is ungrateful, but frequently less culpable of ingratitude than his benefactor.

97. If we believe that mind and judgment are distinct, we are deceived: judgment is merely the breadth of the mind's illumination. This illumination delves into the depths of subjects, notices all that is noticeable, and discerns what seems imperceptible. Hence, we must concur that it is the expanse of the mind's light that generates all the consequences we attribute to judgment.

98. Every individual extols their heart, while none dares to commend their understanding.

99. Politeness of mind entails cultivating pure and refined thoughts.

100. Gallantry of mind is saying the most empty things in an agreeable manner.

101. Ideas often flash across our minds more complete than we could make them after much labour.

102. The head is ever the dupe of the heart.

103. Those who know their minds do not necessarily know their hearts.

104. Men and things have each their proper perspective; to judge rightly of some it is necessary to see them near, of others we can never judge rightly but at a distance.

105. A man for whom accident discovers sense, is not a rational being. A man only is so who understands, who distinguishes, who tests it.

106. To understand matters rightly we should understand their details, and as that knowledge is almost infinite, our knowledge is always superficial and imperfect.

107. One kind of flirtation is to boast we never flirt.

108. The head cannot long play the part of the heart.

109. Youth changes its tastes by the warmth of its blood, age retains its tastes by habit.

110. Nothing is given so profusely as advice.

111. The more we love a woman the more prone we are to hate her.

112. The blemishes of the mind, like those of the face, increase by age.

113. There may be good but there are no pleasant marriages.

114. We are inconsolable at being deceived by our enemies and betrayed by our friends, yet still we are often content to be thus served by ourselves.

115. It is as easy unwittingly to deceive oneself as to deceive others.

116. Nothing is less sincere than the way of asking and giving advice. The person asking seems to pay deference to the opinion of his friend, while thinking in reality of making his friend approve his opinion and be responsible for his conduct. The person giving the advice returns the confidence placed in him by eager and disinterested zeal, in doing which he is usually guided only by his own interest or reputation.

117. The most subtle of our acts is to simulate blindness for snares that we know are set for us. We are never so easily deceived as when trying to deceive.

118. The intention of never deceiving often exposes us to deception.

119. We become so accustomed to disguise ourselves to others that at last we are disguised to ourselves.

120. We often act treacherously more from weakness than from a fixed motive.

121. We frequently do good to enable us with impunity to do evil.

122. If we conquer our passions it is more from their weakness than from our strength.

123. If we never flattered ourselves we should have but scant pleasure.

124. The most deceitful persons spend their lives in blaming deceit, so as to use it on some great occasion to promote some great interest.

125. The daily employment of cunning marks a little mind, it generally happens that those who resort to it in one respect to protect themselves lay themselves open to attack in another.

126. Cunning and treachery are the offspring of incapacity.

127. The true way to be deceived is to think oneself more knowing than others.

128. Too great cleverness is but deceptive delicacy, true delicacy is the most substantial cleverness.

129. It is sometimes necessary to play the fool to avoid being deceived by cunning men.

130. Weakness is the only fault which cannot be cured.

131. The most insignificant failing of women who surrender themselves to love is their capacity to love.

132. It is considerably simpler to display wisdom on behalf of others than to possess it for oneself. Thus the proverb, A man who represents himself in court has a fool for a client.

133. The only exemplary instances worth considering are those that expose the absurdity of flawed originals.

134. We are never as laughable due to our genuine habits as we are due to the affected ones we adopt.

135. At times, we deviate further from our own selves than we do from others.

136. There are some individuals who would never have experienced love if they had never heard it spoken of.

137. When devoid of vanity, we utter fewer words.

138. A person would rather speak ill of themselves than say nothing at all.

139. One of the reasons why we encounter so few rational and engaging conversationalists is that hardly anyone focuses more on what they want to say than on their response to what is being said. The most clever and polite individuals are content with appearing attentive, while we perceive in their minds and eyes that, at that very moment, their thoughts are wandering away from the current conversation and longing to return to what they desire to express. Instead of recognizing that the worst way to persuade or please others is by attempting to please ourselves so strongly, we should understand that active listening and skillful responses are some of the most captivating qualities one can possess in a conversation.

140. If it were not for the company of fools, a witty individual would often find themselves greatly at a loss.

141. We often boast about never experiencing boredom, yet we are so self-absorbed that we fail to realize how frequently we bore others.

142. Just as it is characteristic of great minds to convey much in few words, it is characteristic of small minds to use many words to convey nothing at all.

143. More often than not, we exaggerate the positive qualities of others based on our own emotional estimation rather than their actual merit. When we praise them, we seek to attract their praise in return.

144. We are reluctant to offer praise, and when we do, there is always a motive behind it. Praise is a form of flattery—subtle, artful, and concealed—serving different gratifications for both the one who praises and the one who is praised. The recipient perceives it as a reward for their merit, while the giver bestows it to demonstrate their impartiality and knowledge.

145. We often employ disguised praise that, in its impact on those we extol, reveals faults that could not have been exposed through any other means.

146. Usually, we only praise in order to be praised.

147. Only a few possess the wisdom to prefer constructive criticism, which is beneficial, over treacherous praise.

148. Certain reproaches contain praise, and certain praises contain reproach.

149. The rejection of praise is merely a desire to be praised twice.

150. The desire that compels us to deserve praise strengthens our positive qualities, and the praise bestowed upon wit, valor, and beauty tends to enhance them.

151. It is easier to exert control over others than to avoid being controlled by them.

152. If we never flattered ourselves, the flattery of others would not harm us.

153. Nature bestows merit, but it is fortune that puts it to use.

154. Fortune cures us of many faults that reason alone cannot.

155. There are individuals whose abilities alone repel, and there are individuals who charm even with their faults.

156. There are individuals whose sole merit lies in saying and doing foolish things at the opportune moment, and if they were to alter their behavior, they would ruin everything.

157. The reputation of great individuals should always be assessed based on the methods employed to acquire it.

158. Flattery is counterfeit currency that only our vanity accepts.

159. Having great qualities is not enough; we must also know how to employ them effectively.

160. No matter how brilliant an action may be, it should not be deemed great unless it stems from a noble motive.

161. To gauge the effects produced by actions, there must be a certain harmony between those actions and the accompanying ideas.

162. The art of leveraging moderate abilities to one's advantage garners praise and often gains more renown than genuine brilliance.

163. Countless arts may appear foolish on the surface, while their underlying motives are wise and weighty.

164. It is far simpler to appear suited for roles we do not occupy than for those we do.

165. Ability earns us the esteem of genuine individuals, while luck gains us the favor of the masses.

166. The world often rewards the appearance of merit more than merit itself.

167. Avarice opposes economy more than it does generosity.

168. Despite hope's deceitful nature, it leads us pleasantly through life's journey to the very end. Hope travels through, nor quits us when we die.

169. Idleness and fear keep us on the path of duty, but our virtue often receives the praise.

170. When one acts rightly and honestly, it is difficult to determine whether it is due to integrity or skill.

171. Just as rivers disappear into the sea, virtues become absorbed by self-interest.

172. Upon thorough examination of the varied effects of indifference, we realize that we fail more in our responsibilities than in our personal interests.

173. Curiosity manifests in different forms: one arises from self-interest, which compels us to seek knowledge that benefits us, and another stems from pride, which arises from a desire to possess knowledge that others lack.

174. It is much wiser to accustom our minds to endure the hardships we currently face than to speculate on the potential hardships that may befall us.

175. Constancy in love is a perpetual inconstancy that causes our hearts to attach themselves successively to all the qualities of the person we love, sometimes favoring one, sometimes another. This constancy is merely a fixed inconstancy limited to the same individual.

176. There are two types of constancy in love: one arises from continually discovering new aspects to love in the beloved, and the other stems from regarding constancy as a matter of honor.

177. Perseverance does not warrant blame or praise, as it merely signifies the continuation of tastes and emotions that we cannot create or eradicate.

178. Our affinity for new pursuits is not solely born out of weariness with the old or a desire for change; it is driven by the aspiration to be admired by those more knowledgeable than ourselves and the hope for an advantage over those who know less.

179. We often complain about the levity of our friends as a means to justify our own in advance.

180. Our repentance is not so much sorrow for the wrongs we have committed as it is fear of the misfortune that may befall us.

181. There are two types of inconstancy: one arises from a frivolous or weak mind, causing us to accept everyone's opinion, while the other, which is more forgivable, stems from an excess of options.

182. Vices become intertwined with virtues, like poison mingling with medicine. Prudence combines and blends them, making them beneficial in the face of life's challenges.

183. To uphold the honor of virtue, we must acknowledge that the greatest misfortunes people experience are often the consequences of their own crimes.

184. When we admit our faults, we seek to repair the damage we have caused in the eyes of others through sincerity. However, it is worth noting that we rarely admit our faults except out of vanity.

185. Heroes exist on both sides of the moral spectrum, encompassing both good and evil.

186. We don't despise all individuals with vices, but we do disdain those who lack virtues. As Junius remarked, If individuals have no virtues, their vices may be of use to us.

187. The name of virtue serves our self-interest just as much as the name of vice.

188. The stability of the mind is as uncertain as that of the body. Even when passions seem distant, we remain susceptible to their influence, just as one can fall ill even when in good health.

189. It appears that nature has predetermined the boundaries of our virtues and vices from the moment of our birth.

190. Great men should not possess great faults.

191. Vices follow us throughout our lives, much like the landlords we encounter in our successive lodgings. Even if we were to travel the same path again, our experience would likely not prevent us from encountering them.

192. When our vices depart from us, we often delude ourselves into thinking that we have left them behind.

193. The mind, like the body, experiences relapses in its ailments. What we often perceive as a cure is merely a temporary respite or a shift from one affliction to another.

194. The flaws of the mind are akin to scars on the body. No matter how diligently we tend to them, the marks remain, and there is always a risk of reopening old wounds.

195. The presence of numerous vices often hinders us from abandoning a single one.

196. We easily forget our faults when they are known only to ourselves. As Seneca said, Each person calls himself innocent, looking to the witness rather than to his conscience.

197. There are individuals whom we cannot believe capable of wrongdoing until we witness it firsthand. However, there are very few in whom we would be surprised to see such behavior.

198. To diminish the glory of some individuals, we exaggerate the faults of others. In the case of praising Prince Condé and Marshal Turenne, we would not feel the need to criticize them if we did not wish to blame them both.

199. The desire to appear clever often hinders us from actually being so.

200. Vanity accompanies virtue and aids its advancement.

201. Those who believe they can satisfy the world greatly deceive themselves, but those who believe the world cannot be content without them deceive themselves even more.

202. Dishonestly honest individuals hide their faults from both themselves and others. Truly honest individuals, on the other hand, possess complete self-awareness and willingly confess their shortcomings.

203. True wisdom lies in remaining unruffled by provocations.

204. Women's coldness adds a burden and restraint to their beauty.

205. In women, virtue often manifests as a desire for reputation and tranquility.

206. A genuinely virtuous person desires to withstand the scrutiny of other virtuous individuals.

207. Folly accompanies us throughout our lives. If someone appears wise, it is only because their folly is proportionate to their age and fortune.

208. There are foolish people who are aware of their folly and skillfully use it to their advantage.

209. Those who live without folly are not as wise as they believe themselves to be.

210. As we grow older, we become both more foolish and wiser.

211. Some people are like farces, praised for a while despite being foolish and distasteful.

212.   Most people judge others based solely on their success or fortune.

213.   The love of glory, fear of shame, greed for fortune, desire for a comfortable life, and the tendency to belittle others often motivate the bravery that men boast of.

214.   For common soldiers, displaying valor is a risky way to earn a living.

215.   Perfect bravery and extreme cowardice are two rare extremes. The vast space between them encompasses all other types of courage. The difference between them is as significant as the difference between faces and temperaments. Men may freely expose themselves at the beginning of an action but become easily discouraged if it continues. Some are satisfied with fulfilling worldly honor and do little else. Others are not always equally in control of their fear. Some succumb to panic, while others charge forward because they dare not remain in their positions. There are those whose courage is bolstered by facing small dangers, which prepares them for greater perils. Some dare a sword cut but shy away from a bullet, while others fear bullets little but dread fighting with swords. These various types of courage have one thing in common: during the night, fear intensifies and conceals both courageous and cowardly actions, allowing men to spare themselves. There is also a more general prudence to consider, for we rarely find a man who does everything he would have done if he were assured of escaping unscathed. Therefore, it is certain that the fear of death diminishes valor to some extent.

216.   True bravery is doing privately what one would do publicly.

217.   Intrepidity is an extraordinary strength of the soul that elevates it above the troubles, disorders, and emotions that witnessing great perils can arouse. Heroes with this strength maintain a calm demeanor and preserve their reason and freedom even in the most surprising and terrible accidents.

218.   Hypocrisy is the tribute that vice pays to virtue.

219.   Most people expose themselves in battle only enough to save their honor. Few wish to expose themselves more than necessary or more than is required to achieve their intended goal.

220.   Vanity, shame, and above all, disposition often make men brave and women chaste.

221.   We do not wish to lose our lives, but we do wish to gain glory. This motivates brave men to show more tact and skill in avoiding death than rogues do in preserving their fortunes.

222.   Few individuals, upon reaching old age, do not show signs of physical or mental decline.

223. Gratitude is like the good faith of merchants; it maintains relationships and ensures that we will find people willing to help us, not because paying debts is just, but because it makes borrowing easier.

224. Those who fulfill their debts of gratitude cannot necessarily claim to be truly grateful.

225. False reckoning in matters of gratitude often occurs because the giver and the recipient do not agree on the value of the benefit.

226. Rushing to discharge an obligation can be a form of ingratitude.

227. Lucky people are not adept at correcting their faults; they always believe they are right when fortune supports their vices or follies.

228. Pride refuses to owe, while self-love refuses to pay.

229. The good we receive from someone should lead us to excuse.

230. Example is highly infectious, and our actions, whether good or evil, have a profound impact on others. We tend to imitate virtuous actions out of admiration and emulate them, while our innate inclination towards wrongdoing is unleashed when we witness evil. Shame confines our natural inclination towards evil, but it is through the power of example that it is ultimately liberated.

231. It is a great folly to aspire solely to wisdom. Wisdom, on its own, is not a comprehensive measure of a fulfilling life. There are other qualities and experiences that contribute to our growth and happiness.

232. Regardless of the reasons we attribute to our afflictions, it is often our self-interest or vanity that lies at the root of them. Our suffering is frequently fueled by our personal desires and the need for recognition.

233. In times of affliction, various forms of hypocrisy can emerge. One form involves mourning for someone dear to us while inwardly lamenting our own loss—regretting the individual's positive opinion of us, mourning the loss of comfort, pleasure, and social standing. In this way, the deceased receive credit for the tears shed on behalf of the living. This type of hypocrisy is self-deceptive in nature. Another form is more insidious as it deceives not only ourselves but also those around us. It is the grief of individuals who seek the glory of a noble and everlasting sorrow. Even after time has eroded their genuine grief, they continue to insistently display their tears, sighs, and groans, wearing a solemn countenance, all to convince others that their sorrow will persist until their death. This sad and distressing vanity is often found in ambitious women who, unable to attain

glory through conventional means due to their gender, strive to gain recognition by displaying inconsolable grief.

There is yet another type of tears, originating from trivial sources, which flow easily and cease just as quickly. These tears are shed to gain a reputation for tenderness, to be pitied, and to avoid the disgrace of not weeping.

234. Our stubborn opposition to prevailing opinions is often driven more by pride than ignorance. We resist conforming because we do not want to occupy a lower position, preferring instead to be among the first.

235. We find solace in the misfortunes of our friends when their adversity provides an opportunity for us to demonstrate our affection for them. It allows us to showcase our compassion and support.

236. Even self-love can be deceived by goodness and momentarily forget itself when we engage in acts of service for others. Paradoxically, this is the shortest route to fulfilling our own self-interest, as we subtly and delicately win over everyone by appearing generous while simultaneously benefiting from the transaction.

237. No one should be lauded for their goodness if they lack the strength to be wicked. In many cases, acts of goodness are mere idleness or a reflection of a weak will.

238. Doing too much good to others can be more perilous than wronging them. Excessive benevolence can lead to unintended negative consequences and dependency.

239. The confidence of the great flatters our pride immensely, as we interpret it as a reflection of our worth. However, we often fail to recognize that it is frequently driven by vanity or an inability to keep secrets.

240. Conformity, distinct from beauty, can be described as a symmetry that follows no specific rules. It is a hidden harmony of features that align with the overall appearance and character of an individual.

241. Flirtation lies at the core of a woman's nature, although not all women practice it. Some are restrained by fear, while others abstain due to their principles.

242. We often bore others without realizing it, even when we are convinced that we cannot possibly be boring.

243. Very few things are inherently impossible to achieve. More often than not, it is our lack of commitment and perseverance that hinders success, rather than the absence of means.

244. True mastery lies in understanding the value of things. It is the ability to discern and appreciate their true worth.

245. There is great skill in concealing one's abilities. When others perceive us as possessing only average talents, but we achieve remarkable diplomatic success, it is a testament to our skill in diplomacy.

246. What may appear as generosity is often ambitious disguised, where one disregards small gains to pursue greater interests.

247. The loyalty of most individuals is merely a product of self-love, employed to gain trust, elevate oneself above others, and become entrusted with important matters.

248. Magnanimity disregards everything to win everything. It is the willingness to let go of personal gain or advantage in order to attain greater achievements or victories.

249. Eloquence extends beyond the choice of words. It resides in the tone of voice, gestures, and facial expressions of a speaker. These elements, along with the words themselves, contribute to the overall impact of one's communication.

250. True eloquence lies in expressing precisely what needs to be said, rather than saying everything that could possibly be said. It is about conveying the essential message effectively.

251. Some people's faults complement their personality, while others' virtues bring shame upon them. Our flaws can sometimes contribute to our unique charm, while our virtues may not always align harmoniously with our overall character.

252. Changing one's tastes is a common occurrence, whereas changing one's inclinations is rare.

253. Self-interest motivates both virtues and vices. Our actions are driven by a complex interplay of personal gain and desire.

254. Humility often masks a calculated submission employed to surpass others. It is one of pride's strategies, lowering us temporarily in order to elevate us in the long run. Indeed, pride manifests in various forms and is most effective at deceiving when it disguises itself as humility.

255. Each emotion carries its distinct tone of voice, gestures, and expressions. The harmony of these elements determines whether people appear agreeable or disagreeable.

256. In every profession, we assume a role and appearance to present ourselves as we desire to be perceived. Hence, the world is essentially comprised of actors.

257. Gravity, as a demeanor, is a deliberate physical posture invented to conceal intellectual emptiness or the absence of deep thought.

258. Good taste is cultivated more through judgment than wit. It is the ability to discern and appreciate aesthetics, refinement, and appropriateness.

259. The pleasure of love lies in the act of loving itself. We derive greater happiness from experiencing passion than from merely inspiring it in others.

260. Civility is merely a desire to receive civility in return and to be regarded as polite. It is rooted in the expectation of reciprocal courteous behavior.

261. The education of young people often aims to cultivate a sense of self-love, fostering a strong self-esteem and self-worth.

262. In matters of love, self-love often dominates, and individuals are more inclined to sacrifice the peace and happiness of their loved ones rather than their own.

263. What is often mistaken for generosity is merely the vanity of giving, where the act of giving itself is more appealing than the actual gift.

264. Pity is often a reflection of our own potential misfortunes in the suffering of others. It is a delicate anticipation of the troubles that may befall us. By helping others in similar circumstances, we anticipate the assistance we may require in the future, and the aid we provide becomes a benefit to ourselves.

265. A closed mind breeds stubbornness, and we find it difficult to believe in something that we cannot see.

266. We deceive ourselves if we believe that there are overpowering passions like ambition and love that can conquer all others. Idleness, despite its languishing nature, often assumes mastery. It usurps authority over our plans and actions, gradually eroding both our passions and virtues.

267. A readiness to believe in evil without thorough examination is the result of pride and laziness. We desire to identify the guilty party without bothering to investigate the crime.

268. We attribute base motives to judges, and yet we desire our reputation and fame to depend on the judgment of people who, due to their jealousy, preoccupations, or lack of understanding, are opposed to us. Nevertheless, we go to great lengths to make these individuals decide in our favor, risking our peace and even our lives.

269. No one is clever enough to fully comprehend the extent of the harm they cause.

270. One achieved honor becomes a guarantee for future honors.

271. Youth is a constant state of intoxication; it is a fever of the mind.

272.   The actions taken to acquire great praise should be a source of humiliation for those who receive it. Such actions demonstrate the smallness of their means.

273. There are individuals whom the world approves of, yet their only merit lies in the vices they employ in their affairs.

274. The beauty of novelty is akin to the beauty of a flower compared to the fruit. It possesses a transient luster that easily fades, never to return.

275. Natural goodness, which claims to be evident, is often overshadowed by even the slightest self-interest.

276. Absence extinguishes small passions while inflaming greater ones, just as the wind can blow out a candle and intensify a fire.

277. Women often mistake flirtation for love. The excitement of engaging in a romantic affair, the emotional satisfaction derived from it, the inclination towards being loved, and the difficulty of refusing all persuade them that they experience genuine passion when it is merely a superficial connection.

278. We often become discontented with those who conduct business on our behalf because they frequently prioritize the interests of their trade over the interests of their friends. They seek the honor of succeeding in their chosen endeavors, even if it means abandoning the welfare of their acquaintances.

279. When we exaggerate the kindness shown to us by our friends, it is often less an expression of gratitude and more a desire to showcase our own merits.

280. The praise we give to newcomers is often born out of the envy we harbor for those who are already established.

281. Pride, which can inspire envy, also serves to moderate it.

282.   Some lies, when cleverly disguised, closely resemble truth, making it difficult for us to judge correctly.

283. Knowing how to effectively use good advice can be just as important as giving it.

284. There are wicked individuals who would be far less dangerous if they lacked any shred of goodness.

285. Magnanimity can be adequately defined by its name, although it can be described as the wise pride, the most noble manner of accepting praise.

286. It is impossible to rekindle love for those whom we have genuinely stopped loving.

287. A fertile mind does not provide us with as many options on the same subject as the lack of intelligence makes us hesitate at every idea presented by our imagination, hindering us from initially discerning which one is the best.

288. Certain matters and ailments worsen when remedies are applied at specific times; true expertise lies in knowing when it is perilous to use them.

289. Feigned simplicity is a refined form of deception.

290. There are as many flaws in temperament as there are in the mind.

291. The merit of a person, like the harvest, has its season.

292. Temperament, like many buildings, can be viewed from various angles, some pleasant and others disagreeable.

293. Moderation cannot claim the merit of opposing and conquering Ambition, as they are never found together. Moderation is the lethargy and apathy of the soul, while Ambition is its activity and fervor.

294. We always appreciate those who admire us, but we don't always admire those whom we appreciate.

295. It is fortunate that we are unaware of all our desires.

296. Loving those we do not respect is challenging, but it is equally difficult to love those whom we hold in much higher esteem than ourselves.

297. Bodily temperaments follow a common course and rule that subtly affect our will. They progress in combination and gradually exert a hidden influence over us, to the point that, without our awareness, they become a significant part of all our actions.

298. The gratitude of most individuals is merely a concealed desire to receive greater favors. [Hence the common proverb Gratitude is merely a lively sense of favors to come.]

299. Almost everyone takes pleasure in repaying small debts; many people express gratitude for trivial matters, yet there is scarcely anyone who does not show ingratitude for significant favors.

300. There are follies that are as contagious as diseases.

301. Many people despise, but few know how to generously distribute wealth.

302. Only in matters of little value are we usually bold enough not to rely on appearances.

303. Whatever good quality is attributed to us, we ourselves find nothing new in it.

304. We may forgive those who bore us, but we cannot forgive those whom we bore.

305. Interest, which is accused of all our wrongdoings, often deserves praise for our good deeds.

306. We encounter very few ungrateful individuals when we are capable of bestowing favors.

307. It is as appropriate to boast alone as it is ridiculous to do so in company.

308. Moderation is portrayed as a virtue to restrict the ambition of the great, to console ordinary people for their limited fortune and equally limited ability.

309. There are individuals destined to be fools, who commit foolish acts not only by choice but are compelled by fortune to do so.

310. Sometimes there are incidents in our lives that require a touch of folly to skillfully extricate ourselves.

311. If there are men whose folly has never been evident, it is because it has never been closely examined.

312. Lovers never tire of each other; they always speak of themselves.

313. Why is it that our memory is capable of retaining the most trivial details of our experiences, yet not proficient enough to recall how many times we have recounted them to the same person? Old men who yet retain the memory of things past, and forget how often they have told them, are most tedious companions.

314. The immense pleasure we derive from talking about ourselves should remind us that it is not shared by those who listen.

315. What often prevents us from revealing the depths of our hearts to our friends is not the distrust we have in them but the mistrust we have in ourselves.

316. Weak individuals cannot be sincere.

317. It is a minor misfortune to assist an ungrateful person, but it is unbearable to be obliged by a scoundrel.

318. We may find ways to cure a fool of their folly, but there are none to rectify a person with a stubborn and contrary disposition.

319. If we choose to dwell on the faults of our friends and benefactors, we cannot maintain the sentiments we should hold toward them for long.

320. To praise princes for virtues they do not possess is essentially reproaching them with impunity. Praise undeserved is satire in disguise and in some cases, exaggerated or inappropriate praise becomes the most severe satire.

321. We are closer to loving those who hate us than those who love us more than we desire.

322. Those who fear to be despised are the only ones deserving of contempt.

323. Our wisdom is just as vulnerable to the whims of Fortune as our material possessions.

324. Jealousy contains more self-love than love itself.

325. Often, we console ourselves with the insignificance of evils, for which reason lacks the strength to comfort us.

326. Ridicule brings more dishonor than dishonor itself.

327. We confess to minor faults to convince others that we lack major ones.

328. Envy is more irreconcilable than hatred.

329. Sometimes, we believe that we hate flattery when, in reality, we simply dislike the manner in which it is delivered.

330. We forgive to the extent that we love.

331. It is more challenging to remain faithful to a mistress when one is happy than when one is mistreated by her.

332. Women are not fully aware of all their powers of flirtation.

333. Women cannot exhibit complete severity unless they harbor hatred.

334. Women find it more difficult to renounce flirtations than love.

335. In love, deceit almost always surpasses mistrust.

336. There exists a kind of love in which excess precludes jealousy.

337. Just as there are senses, there are certain good qualities that go unnoticed by those who lack them.

338. When our hatred is too intense, it places us beneath those whom we hate.

339. We can only appreciate our good or evil to the extent of our self-love.

340. The wit of most women tends to reinforce their folly rather than their reason. [Women have an entertaining tattle, and sometimes wit, but for solid reasoning and good sense, I never knew one in my life that had it, and who reasoned and acted consequentially for four and twenty hours together.—Lord Chesterfield, Letter 129.]

341. The heat of youth is no more opposed to safety than the coldness of old age.

342. The accent of our native country resides not only on our tongues but also in our hearts and minds.

343. To become a great person, one must know how to benefit from every turn of fortune.

344. Most men, like plants, possess hidden qualities that chance reveals.

345. Opportunity introduces us to others, but it reveals even more about ourselves.

346. If a woman's temper is uncontrollable, it signifies a lack of control over her mind and heart.

347. We seldom find individuals of good sense except those who agree with us.

348. When one is in love, even the things we firmly believe are doubted.

349. The greatest miracle of love is to eradicate flirtation.

350. We harbor such bitter animosity towards those who deceive us because they consider themselves more cunning than we are.

351. Ending a relationship when love no longer exists is a challenging task.

352. We often find ourselves bored with individuals with whom we should not be bored.

353. A gentleman can love passionately but not like a beast.

354. Certain defects, when masked by a polished exterior, glitter as if they were virtues themselves.

355. Sometimes, we lose friends whose loss brings us greater regret than grief, while others elicit greater grief than regret.

356. We genuinely praise only those who admire us.

357. Small-minded individuals are wounded by trifles, while great minds remain unscathed even by significant matters.

358. Humility is the true manifestation of Christian virtues; without it, our faults persist, concealed by pride from others and often from ourselves.

359. Infidelity should extinguish love, and we should not be jealous when we have valid reasons to be. No one escapes inciting jealousy from those capable of being stirred by it.

360. We feel more humiliated by the slightest infidelity towards us than by our most significant betrayals towards others.

361. Jealousy is always born with love but does not always perish with it.

362. Most women mourn the death of their lovers not solely for the sake of love but to prove themselves deserving of being loved.

363. The harm we inflict upon others brings us less pain than the harm we inflict upon ourselves.

364. We are well aware that it is in poor taste to discuss our wives, but we are not equally aware that the same applies to speaking about ourselves.

365. There are virtues that degenerate into vices when they arise from our nature, and others that, when acquired, are never perfect. For example, reason should teach us to manage our wealth and our trust, while nature should have endowed us with goodness and valor.

366. No matter how skeptical we are of others' sincerity, we always believe they are more sincere with us than with others.

367. There are few virtuous women who do not grow weary of their roles.

368. The majority of good women are like hidden treasures, remaining secure until someone searches for them.

369. The efforts we exert to escape love often inflict greater cruelty upon us than the cruelty of those we love.

370. There are not many cowards who fully comprehend the extent of their fear.

371. The fault of the loved one is often not perceiving when love ceases.

372. Young people often mistake their boorish and rude behavior for naturalness.

373. Deceiving others can sometimes lead to self-deception, with tears as the aftermath.

374. If we believe we love a woman for who she truly is, we are greatly deceived.

375. Ordinary men commonly condemn what is beyond their understanding.

376. True friendship destroys envy, and true love eliminates flirtation.

377. The greatest mistake of insight is not falling short but going too far.

378. We can offer advice, but we cannot inspire conduct in others.

379. As our merit declines, so does our taste.

380. Fortune reveals our virtues or vices, much like light reveals objects.

381. The struggle to remain faithful to someone we love is scarcely better than infidelity.

382. Our actions resemble the rhymed ends of blank verses (Bouts-Rimés) where everyone puts their own interpretation.

383. Talking about ourselves and presenting our faults in the desired light is a significant aspect of sincerity.

384. We should be amazed that we can still be amazed.

385. It is equally challenging to find contentment when one has too much or too little love.

386. Those who refuse to admit they are wrong are often the ones who are frequently mistaken.

387. A fool lacks the substance required to be good.

388. Vanity may not eradicate all virtues, but it certainly undermines them.

389. The vanity of others becomes unbearable when it wounds our own.

390. We are more willing to relinquish our interests than our taste.

391. Fortune appears particularly blind to those whom she has not favored.

392. We should manage fortune like we do our health—enjoy it when it is good, be patient when it is bad, and resort to drastic remedies only in extreme situations.

393. Awkwardness can sometimes disappear in the camp but never in the court.

394. A man may be more clever than some individuals, but not more so than everyone else.

395. Being deceived by someone we loved often brings less unhappiness than being deceived in general.

396. We hold onto our first lover for a long time—if we don't find a second.

397. Though we lack the courage to admit it openly, we are not far from believing that we have no faults and our enemies possess no good qualities.

398. Among all our faults, idleness is the one we most readily acknowledge. We believe it renders all virtues ineffective and, at the very least, suspends their operation.

399. There exists a kind of greatness that does not depend on fortune. It is a certain manner that distinguishes us and seems to destine us for great things. It is the value we unconsciously place upon ourselves, the quality that garners deference from others, and often elevates us above them, surpassing birth, rank, or even merit itself.

400. Talent can exist without position, but there is no position without some form of talent.

401. Rank is to merit what dress is to a pretty woman.

402. In flirtation, love is often the element found in the smallest measure.

403. Fortune sometimes exploits our faults to elevate us, and there are individuals so tiresome that their absence becomes a sought-after reward.

404. It seems that nature has concealed talents and abilities within the depths of our hearts, unknown to us. Only through the power of passions are they brought to light, sometimes providing us with views more genuine and perfect than art could ever achieve.

405. We often reach different stages of life without much experience, despite the number of years we have lived. [To most men experience is like the stern lights of a ship which illumine only the track it has passed.—Coleridge.]

406. Flirts consider it a matter of honor to be jealous of their lovers and conceal their envy of other women.

407. Those who have deceived us with their tricks may not appear as foolish to us as we ourselves seem when ensnared by the tricks of others.

408. The most dangerous folly for older individuals who were once loveable is to forget that they are no longer perceived as such. [Every woman who is not absolutely ugly

thinks herself handsome. The suspicion of age no woman, let her be ever so old, forgives.—Lord Chesterfield, Letter 129.]

409. We would often feel ashamed of even our best actions if the world could see the true motives behind them.

410. The greatest effort of friendship is not to expose our friend's faults but to make them aware of their own.

4ll. Few faults are more excusable than the means we adopt to hide them.

412. It is almost always within our power to re-establish our character, no matter the disgrace we may have deserved. [This is hardly a period at which the most irregular character may not be redeemed. The mistakes of one sin find a retreat in patriotism, those of the other in devotion.—Junius, Letter To The King.]

413. A man who possesses only one kind of wit cannot please for long.

414. Idiots and lunatics are blinded by their own wit.

415. Wit sometimes allows us to act rudely without facing consequences.

416. The vivacity that increases in old age is often closely associated with folly.

417. The quickest cure in love is always the best.

418. Young women who wish not to appear as flirts and old men who wish not to appear ridiculous should refrain from discussing love as if it were of any interest to them.

419. We may seem great in a position beneath our capabilities, but more often than not, we seem small in a position above them.

420. We often mistake debasement for constancy in misfortune and suffer misfortunes without acknowledging them, akin to cowards who fear defending themselves.

421. Conceit causes more conversation than wit.

422. All passions make us commit some faults, but love alone makes us ridiculous. In love we all are fools alike.

423. Few know how to be old.

424. We often credit ourselves with vices opposite to our own; thus, when weak, we boast of our obstinacy.

425. Penetration has a spice of divination in it, which tickles our vanity more than any other quality of the mind.

426. The charm of novelty and old custom, however opposite to each other, equally blind us to the faults of our friends. Two things the most opposite blind us equally, custom and novelty.

427. Most friends sicken us of friendship, and most devotees sicken us of devotion.

428. We easily forgive in our friends those faults we do not perceive.

429. Women who love pardon great indiscretions more readily than little infidelities.

430. In the old age of love, as in life, we still endure the evils, though no longer the pleasures. The youth of friendship is better than its old age.

431. Nothing prevents us from being unaffected so much as our desire to seem so.

432. To praise good actions heartily is, in some measure, to take part in them.

433. The most certain sign of being born with great qualities is to be born without envy.

434. When our friends have deceived us, we owe them only indifference to the tokens of their friendship; yet for their misfortunes, we always owe them pity.

435. Luck and temper rule the world.

436. It is far easier to know men than to know man.

437. We should not judge a man's merit solely by his great abilities, but by the use he makes of them.

438. There is a certain lively gratitude that not only releases us from benefits received but also renders our friends indebted to us by making a return to them as payment. [And understood not that a grateful mind, By owing owes not, but is at once Indebted and discharged.—Milton, Paradise Lost.]

439. We should earnestly desire but few things if we clearly knew what we desired.

440. The reason why the majority of women are so little given to friendship is that it becomes insipid after having felt love. Those who have experienced a great passion neglect friendship, and those who have united themselves to friendship have nought to do with love.

441. As in friendship, so in love, we are often happier from ignorance than from knowledge.

442. We try to make a virtue of vices we are reluctant to correct.

443. The most violent passions provide some respite, but vanity always disturbs us.

444. Old fools are more foolish than young fools.

445. Weakness is more hostile to virtue than vice.

446. What makes the grief of shame and jealousy so acute is that vanity cannot aid us in enduring them.

447. Propriety is the least of all laws but the most obeyed. Honour has its supreme laws, to which education is bound to conform....Those things which honour forbids are more rigorously forbidden when the laws do not concur in the prohibition, and those it commands are more strongly insisted upon when they happen not to be commanded by law.

448. A well-trained mind has less difficulty in submitting to than in guiding an ill-trained mind.

449. When fortune surprises us by giving us some great office without having gradually led us to expect it or without having raised our hopes, it is nearly impossible to occupy it well and to appear worthy to fill it.

450. Our pride is often increased by what we suppress from our other faults. [The loss of sensual pleasures was supplied and compensated by spiritual pride.—Gibbon, Decline And Fall, chap. xv.]

451. No fools are as wearisome as those who have some wit.

452. No one believes that in every respect he is inferior to the man he considers the most capable in the world.

453. In great matters, we should not try so much to create opportunities as to utilize those that present themselves.

454. There are few occasions when we should make a bad bargain by giving up the good on condition that no ill is said of us.

455. However disposed the world may be to judge wrongly, it far more often favors false merit than does justice to true.

456. Sometimes we encounter a fool with wit, but never one with discretion.

457. We would gain more by letting the world see what we are than by trying to seem what we are not.

458. Our enemies come closer to the truth in the opinions they form of us than we do in our opinion of ourselves.

459. There are many remedies to cure love, yet none are infallible.

460. It would be well for us if we knew all the actions our passions make us do.

461. Age, a tyrant, forbids the pleasures of youth under penalty of life.

462. The pride that criticizes faults we believe ourselves free from also despises the virtues we lack.

463. In our grief for our enemies' miseries, there is often more pride than genuine compassion—a display of our superiority.

464. There exists an incomprehensible excess of good and evil.

465. Innocence is fortunate if it receives the same protection as crime.

466. Among all the passionate emotions, love becomes women the most.

467. Vanity often leads us to betray our taste rather than reason.

468. Certain negative qualities can form great talents.

469. Our genuine desires rarely align with our rational desires.

470. All our qualities, good or bad, are uncertain and subject to circumstance.

471. In their first love, women love their lovers; in subsequent loves, they love the idea of love.

472. Pride, like other passions, has its follies. We're ashamed to admit jealousy, yet we take pride in being able to feel it.

473. True friendship is rarer than true love.

474. Only a few women's charm survives their beauty.

475. The desire to be pitied or admired often dominates our confidence.

476. Our envy outlasts the happiness of those we envy.

477. The same strength of character that allows us to resist love also makes our resistance enduring. Weak individuals, constantly consumed by passions, seldom possess true strength.

478. Imagination cannot conceive as many contradictions as naturally exist in every heart.

479. True gentleness can only be possessed by those with firmness. In those who appear gentle, it is usually weakness that can easily turn into harshness.

480. Blaming timidity in those we wish to cure is a dangerous fault.

481. Genuine good-nature is a rarity; those who believe they possess it are often merely pliant or weak.

482. The mind gravitates toward idleness and habit, attaching itself to what is easy or pleasurable. This habit limits our knowledge, as few make the effort to expand their minds to their full capacity.

483. We are often more satirical out of vanity than malice.

484. When the heart still carries remnants of a passion, it is more prone to embracing a new one than when fully cured.

485. Those who have experienced great passions often find their lives miserable in the process of being cured.

486. There are more people without self-love than without envy.

487. Idleness is more prevalent in the mind than in the body.

488. The tranquility or disturbance of our minds depends not so much on what we consider significant in life but on how well we manage the little daily occurrences.

489. Even wicked people dare not openly appear as enemies of virtue; instead, they either pretend it is false or attribute crimes to it when they wish to persecute it.

490. Love often transitions to ambition, but rarely does ambition revert back to love.

491. Extreme avarice is often misguided; it is a passion far from its mark, easily swayed by present circumstances to the detriment of the future.

492. Avarice often produces contradictory results: some sacrifice their possessions for uncertain and distant expectations, while others mistake great future gains for small present interests.

493. Men seem to believe they lack enough faults, so they cultivate certain artificial qualities that eventually become ingrained faults, beyond correction.

494. Men's acute self-awareness of their faults becomes evident when they speak of their conduct; their self-love, which usually blinds them, also enlightens them, enabling them to suppress or disguise any potential criticisms.

495. Young men embarking on life should either be shy or bold; a serious and sedate demeanor often devolves into impertinence.

496. Quarrels would be brief if fault lay only on one side.

497. Being young is of little value to a woman unless she is also pretty, and being pretty holds little worth without youth.

498. Some individuals are so frivolous and fickle that they lack genuine flaws as much as substantial qualities.

499. A woman's first flirtation is not truly counted until she has had a second.

500. Certain individuals are so self-absorbed that when in love, they find a way to be consumed by the passion itself rather than the person they love.

501. Love, though delightful, pleases us more through its expressions than its essence.

502. A little wit combined with good sense becomes less tiresome in the long run than abundant wit accompanied by ill-nature.

503. Jealousy is the worst of all evils, yet those who cause it rarely receive pity.

504. Thus, having discussed the shallowness of numerous apparent virtues, it is only fair to address the shallowness of contempt for death. I refer to that disdain for death which the heathens boasted of deriving solely from their unaided understanding, without any hope of an afterlife. There is a distinction between facing death with courage and despising it. The former is quite common, while I believe the latter is always feigned. Despite numerous arguments that have been presented to convince us that death is not an evil, and even though the weakest of men, as well as the bravest, have set many noble examples upon which such an opinion could be based, I do not think that any sensible person has truly believed in it. The efforts we make to persuade both ourselves and others clearly demonstrate that the task is far from easy. We may become disgusted with life for various reasons, but we cannot despise it. Even those who commit suicide do not regard it lightly and are just as alarmed and startled as the rest of the world if death approaches them in a different manner than they had chosen. The difference we observe in the

courage of a great number of brave individuals arises from encountering death in a manner different from what they had imagined, when it reveals itself closer at one time than at another. Consequently, it often happens that having despised death when they were ignorant of it, they fear it once they become acquainted with it. If we could avoid witnessing it in all its circumstances, we might perhaps believe that it is not the greatest of evils. The wisest and bravest are those who take the best measures to avoid contemplating it, as every person who sees it in its true light regards it as dreadful. The inevitability of death gave birth to the constancy of philosophers. They deemed it fitting to depart gracefully when they could not evade their fate, and since they could not prolong their lives indefinitely, their only recourse was to construct an immortal reputation and salvage whatever they could from the general wreckage. To put on a brave face, it is enough not to express all that we think to ourselves and to rely more on our nature than on our fallible reason, which might lead us to believe that we can approach death with indifference. The glory of dying courageously, the hope of being mourned, the desire to leave behind a good reputation, the assurance of being freed from the miseries of life and no longer being subject to the whims of fortune—these are resources that should not be disregarded. However, we must not regard them as infallible. They should affect us to the same extent as a single shelter affects those who storm a fortress in times of war. From a distance, they believe it may provide cover, but when they draw near, they find it to be a feeble protection. It is merely self-deception to imagine that death, when near, will appear the same as when it is distant, or that our feelings, which are inherently weak, are naturally so strong that they will not suffer under the harshest of trials. It is equally absurd to test the power of self-esteem and assume it will enable us to disregard what will inevitably destroy it. And the mind, in which we place so much trust to find numerous resources, will prove too feeble in the struggle to convince us as we desire. For it is this very mind that often betrays us, revealing not contempt for death, but rather all that is terrifying and dreadful about it. The most it can do for us is to persuade us to turn our gaze away and fix it upon other matters. Cato and Brutus each chose noble distractions. Some time ago, a lackey contented himself by dancing on the scaffold when he was about to be subjected to the wheel. Thus, despite the diversity of motives, they all achieve the same outcome. Furthermore, it is a fact that regardless of the difference between a nobleman and a peasant, we have consistently witnessed both facing death with equal composure. However, there is always this distinction: the nobleman's contempt for death is merely the love of fame that obscures death from his sight, while in the peasant, it is merely the consequence of his limited vision that shields him from the magnitude of the evil and allows him to reflect on other things.

Miscellaneous

I. Self-love, or the love of self and all things for one's own sake, engenders self-centeredness, leading individuals to worship themselves and, if circumstances allow, to exert tyranny over others. It is a relentless force, seeking fulfillment outside of itself and resting momentarily on external matters, akin to a bee extracting nectar from flowers. Its desires are obstinate, its intentions well-concealed, and its manipulation skills unmatched. Its adaptability is indescribable, surpassing even the transformations of metamorphosis and the intricacies of chemistry. Its depths and intricacies are unfathomable, evading even the most perceptive gaze, shrouded in countless imperceptible layers. It often remains invisible to itself, harboring countless loves and hatreds, some so monstrous that it disowns them when exposed, unable to admit their existence. In the darkness that envelops it, ludicrous convictions about itself are born, giving rise to errors, ignorance, and foolish blunders. It deludes itself into believing that dormant passions are deceased and convinces itself that it has lost all appetite for that which it has grown satiated with.

However, this dense veil of self-deception does not obstruct its perception of external matters, much like our eyes that can observe everything but their own form. Indeed, in significant and pressing affairs, when the intensity of its desires consumes its attention, it perceives, feels, hears, imagines, suspects, penetrates, and divines everything. Each passion seems to possess its own magical power. Its attachments are both close and unyielding, futilely attempting to sever them even in the face of imminent misfortune. Yet, on occasion, it effortlessly achieves what it failed to accomplish despite exerting its entire force over the course of years. This suggests that it is self-love itself that fuels its desires rather than the intrinsic beauty and merit of its objects. It embellishes and magnifies them through its own subjective lens. It becomes the game it pursues, eagerly chasing after that which itself covets. Self-love is a paradoxical entity, embodying opposites. It is imperious and obedient, sincere and false, compassionate and cruel, timid and bold. Its desires fluctuate according to temperaments, oscillating between riches and pleasures. It morphs with our age, fortune, and aspirations. It remains indifferent to whether it possesses many or few objects, for it can fragment itself into multiple parts or consolidate into a singular focus at its whim.

Inconstant by nature, self-love exhibits countless changes arising from diverse sources, along with an infinity of transformations originating from within its own being. Its inconsistency stems from fickleness, frivolity, infatuation with novelty, weariness, and disinterest. It is capricious, engrossing itself intensely and laboriously in obtaining things of minimal utility, sometimes even detrimental, solely because it desires them. It can be foolish, directing its entire devotion to the most trivial matters. It derives pleasure from the most mundane affairs and takes pride in the most contemptible. It manifests in all states and conditions of life, omnipresent and all-consuming. It sustains itself on everything and nothing, adapting to both the presence and absence of things. It aligns itself even with those who oppose it, entering into their schemes, and astonishingly, it despises itself alongside them. It conspires against its own well-being, working toward its own ruin. In essence, concerned solely with its own existence and ensuring its continuation, it becomes its own adversary. Hence, it is not surprising to find it occasionally united with severe austerity or willingly partnering in its own destruction. When eradicated in one aspect, it reestablishes itself elsewhere. Even in surrender, it revels in its own defeat. Thus, this is the portrait of self-love, an incessant tumult that permeates our entire lives. It resembles the sea, with its constant ebb and flow, faithfully mirroring the stormy succession of thoughts and perpetual motion within.

II. The passions are merely varying degrees of the warmth or coldness of one's blood.

III. Moderation in times of prosperity arises from the fear of the shame that accompanies arrogance or the dread of losing what we possess.

IV. Moderation is akin to temperance in eating; we could consume more, but we fear the consequences of overindulgence and falling ill.

V. Each person finds in others the very faults they deem worthy of condemnation within themselves.

VI. Pride, weary of its artifices and manifold transformations, eventually reveals its true face through haughtiness. Haughtiness, therefore, becomes the explicit manifestation and outward expression of pride. Indeed, haughtiness is pride unmasked.

VII. One form of happiness lies in precisely knowing the extent to which we can endure misery.

VIII. If we cannot find inner peace within ourselves, seeking it elsewhere is futile.

IX. One should be accountable for their own fortune, thus enabling them to be responsible for their future actions

X. Love is to the soul of the lover what the soul is to the body it animates.

XI. Since one is never free to choose whether to love or cease loving, the lover cannot justly complain about the fickleness of their beloved, nor can the beloved reproach the lover for their inconstancy.

XII. Justice in those judges who display moderation is merely a love for their position of authority.

XIII. When we grow weary of loving, we find contentment in the faithlessness of our beloved, as it releases us from our own fidelity.

XIV. The initial joy we experience at the happiness of our friends does not stem from innate goodness or friendship itself. It is rather a result of self-love, which flatters us by suggesting that our turn for good fortune will come or that we will benefit from the prosperity of our friends.

XV. Even in the misfortune of our closest friends, we often discover something that does not entirely displease us.

XVI. How can we expect others to keep our secrets if we do not keep them ourselves?

XVII. As if self-love's ability to change itself were not enough, it also possesses the power to alter other objects in astonishing ways. It not only disguises them so effectively that it deceives itself but also transforms the state and nature of things. For instance, when a woman harbors animosity toward us and directs her hatred and persecution our way, self-love renders harsh judgments upon her actions, exaggerating her faults to an enormous degree. It casts her good qualities in such an unfavorable light that they become more displeasing than her faults. However, if the same woman becomes favorably inclined toward us or if our shared interests reconcile us, our self-interest restores her lost luster. The negative aspects fade away, and her positive traits shine with renewed brilliance. We even summon great indulgence to justify the conflict she waged against us. While this truth is evident in all passions, it is most clearly exhibited in love. We witness a lover consumed by rage due to neglect or infidelity from the beloved, contemplating the most vengeful acts inspired by their passion. Yet, as soon as the sight of their beloved calms the storm within, their passion deems that beauty innocent. They only accuse themselves, condemn their own condemnations, and through the miraculous power of self-love, they absolve their beloved of even the darkest deeds, taking all blame upon themselves. (No specific date or number provided for this maxim.)

XVIII. The lazy exert the greatest pressure upon others when they have appeased their idleness and seek to appear industrious.

XIX. The blindness of individuals is the most perilous consequence of their pride. It seems to nurture and amplify pride, depriving us of knowledge of remedies that could alleviate our miseries and correct our faults.

XX. We are least justified in despairing of finding reason in others when we ourselves lack it.

XXI. Crimes have not been diminished by the precepts of philosophers, and Seneca, above all, has used them to build up pride.

XXII. Not perceiving the growing coolness of our friends is proof of little friendship.

XXIII. The most wise may be wise in indifferent and ordinary matters, but they are seldom wise in their most serious affairs.

XXIV. The most subtle folly emerges from the most subtle wisdom

XXV. Sobriety is the love of health or an incapacity to eat much.

XXVI. We remember things best when we are tired of talking about them.

XXVII. The praise bestowed upon us is at least useful in firmly establishing our practice of virtue.

XXVIII. Self-love takes care to prevent the person we flatter from becoming the one who flatters us the most.

XXIX. Men only blame vice and praise virtue out of interest.

XXX. We make no distinction in the kinds of anger, although there is a light and almost innocent anger that arises from complexion and temperament, and another very criminal anger, which is, to speak properly, the fury of pride.

XXXI. Great souls are not those who have fewer passions and more virtues than the common people, but those who have greater designs.

XXXII. Kings treat men as they do pieces of money; they assign them whatever value they desire, and one is forced to accept them according to their assigned worth and not their true value.

XXXIII. Natural ferocity makes fewer people cruel than self-love.

XXXIV. One can say of all our virtues what an Italian poet says about the propriety of women, that it is often merely the art of appearing chaste.

XXXV. There are crimes that become innocent and even glorious due to their brilliance, their number, or their excess. Thus, public robbery is called financial skill, and the unjust capture of provinces is called a conquest.

XXXVI. One never finds in man good or evil in excess.

XXXVII. Those who are incapable of committing great crimes do not easily suspect others.

XXXVIII. The pomp of funerals concerns the vanity of the living more than the honor of the dead.

XXXIX. Despite the variety and change in the world, we can observe a secret chain and a regulated order of all time by Providence, which ensures that everything follows its proper sequence and falls into its destined course.

XL. Intrepidity should sustain the heart in conspiracies instead of valor, as it alone provides the necessary firmness for the perils of war.

XLI. Those who attempt to define victory by her birth will be tempted to imitate the poets and call her the Daughter of Heaven, since they cannot find her origin on earth. Truly, victory is produced from an infinity of actions that, instead of intending to beget her, only seek the particular interests of their masters. All those who compose an army, in pursuing their own rise and glory, bring about a good that is so great and general.

XLII. A man who has never been in danger cannot vouch for his courage.

XLIII. We more often set limits to our gratitude than to our desires and hopes.

XLIV. Imitation is always unhappy, for all that is counterfeit displeases us with the very things that charm us when they are original.

XLV. We do not mourn the loss of our friends based on their merits, but according to our own needs and the opinion we believed we had impressed upon them of our worth.

XLVI. It is very difficult to separate the general goodness spread all over the world from great cleverness.

XLVII. For us to always be good, others should believe that they cannot behave wickedly towards us without consequences.

XLVIII. Having confidence in our ability to please often becomes an infallible means of being displeasing.

XLIX. The confidence we have in ourselves largely arises from the confidence we have in others.

L. There is a general revolution that changes the tastes of the mind as well as the fortunes of the world.

LI. Truth is the foundation and the reason for the perfection of beauty, for no matter the stature of a thing, it cannot be beautiful and perfect unless it truly embodies what it should be and possesses all that it should have.

LII. There are fine things that shine more brilliantly when unfinished than when excessively completed.

LIII. Magnanimity is a noble effort of pride that enables a person to master themselves in order to become the master of all things

LIV. Luxury and overly refined policies in states are a sure sign of their impending downfall, as all factions, pursuing their own interests, turn away from the public good.

LV. Among all passions, idleness is the least known to us. She is the most ardent and wicked of all, even though her violence may be imperceptible and the evils she causes concealed. If we carefully consider her power, we shall find that in every encounter, she becomes the mistress of our sentiments, our interests, and our pleasures. Like the fabled Remora, she can halt the mightiest vessels. She is a hidden rock, more perilous in the most important matters than sudden squalls and the most violent tempests. The repose of idleness is a magical charm that abruptly suspends the most fervent pursuits and the most stubborn resolutions. In fact, to truly understand this passion, we must acknowledge that idleness, like a state of bliss for the soul, consoles us for all losses and fills the void of all our wants.

LVI. We have a great fondness for deciphering the characters of others, but we dislike being deciphered ourselves.

LVII. What a tiresome ailment it is that compels one to preserve their health through a strict regimen.

LVIII. It is much easier to fall in love when one is free than to rid oneself of it after falling.

LIX. Women mostly surrender themselves out of weakness rather than passion. Hence, it is bold and assertive men who often succeed better than others, despite not being as lovable.

LX. Not loving is an infallible means of being loved in love.

LXI. The demand for sincerity from both lovers and mistresses when they cease to love each other arises not so much from a desire to be alerted to the cessation of love, but rather from a longing to be assured that they are still beloved, even when it is not denied.

LXII. The most fitting comparison for love is that of a fever, over which we have no control regarding its intensity or duration.

LXIII. The greatest skill of the least skilled is to know how to submit to the guidance of another.

LXIV. We always fear encountering those whom we love when we have been flirting with others.

LXV. We should console ourselves for our faults when we possess enough strength to admit them.

LXVI. Interest is the soul of self-love, inasmuch as when the body deprived of its soul is without sight, feeling or knowledge, without thought or movement, so self-love, riven so to speak from its interest, neither sees, nor hears, nor smells, nor moves; thus it is that the same man who will run over land and sea for his own interest becomes suddenly paralyzed when engaged for that of others; from this arises that sudden dulness and, as it were, death, with which we afflict those to whom we speak of our own matters; from this also their sudden resurrection when in our narrative we relate something concerning them; from this we find in our conversations and business that a man becomes dull or bright just as his own interest is near to him or distant from him.

LXVII. Why we cry out so much against maxims which lay bare the heart of man, is because we fear that our own heart shall be laid bare.

LXVIII. Hope and fear are inseparable.

LXIX. It is a common thing to hazard life to escape dishonour; but, when this is done, the actor takes very little pain to make the enterprise succeed in which he is engaged, and certain it is that they who hazard their lives to take a city or to conquer a province are better officers, have more merit, and wider and more useful, views than they who merely expose themselves to vindicate their honour; it is very common to find people of the latter class, very rare to find those of the former.

LXX. The taste changes, but the will remains the same.

LXXI. The power which women whom we love have over us is greater than that which we have over ourselves.

LXXII. That which makes us believe so easily that others have defects is that we all so easily believe what we wish

LXXIII. I am perfectly aware that good sense and fine wit are tedious to every age, but tastes are not always the same, and what is good at one time will not seem so at another. This makes me think that few persons know how to be old.

LXXIV. God has permitted, to punish man for his original sin, that he should be so fond of his self-love, that he should be tormented by it in all the actions of his life.

LXXV. And so far it seems to me the philosophy of a lacquey can go; I believe that all gaiety in that state of life is very doubtful indeed.

LXXVI. - Many individuals desire to be devout, but no one wishes to be humble.

LXXVII. - The labor of the body liberates us from the burdens of the mind, thus bringing happiness to the poor.

LXXVIII. - True penitential sorrows (mortifications) are those that remain unknown; vanity easily mitigates the others.

LXXIX. - Humility is the altar upon which God desires us to offer Him sacrifices.

LXXX. - A wise man requires only a few things to be happy, while nothing can satisfy a fool; hence, most men are miserable.

LXXXI. - Our efforts are more focused on appearing happy to others rather than seeking true happiness.

LXXXII. - Extinguishing the initial desire is easier than satisfying the subsequent ones.

LXXXIII. - Wisdom is to the soul what health is to the body.

LXXXIV. - The powerful individuals of the world cannot command physical well-being or mental peace, and they often acquire their possessions at an excessive cost.

LXXXV. - Before strongly desiring something, we should examine the happiness of those who already possess it.

LXXXVI. - A genuine friend is the most valuable possession, even though we may not actively seek to acquire it.

LXXXVII. - Lovers do not wish to acknowledge the faults of their partners until their enchantment fades away.

LXXXVIII. - Prudence and love are incompatible; as love intensifies, prudence diminishes.

LXXXIX. - It can be pleasing for a husband to have a jealous wife, as he constantly hears her speaking about the beloved object.

XC. - A woman who possesses both virtue and love is truly deserving of pity.

XCI. - A wise man finds it better to avoid a conflict than to emerge victorious.

XCII. - Studying people is more essential than studying books. The proper study of mankind is man.

XCIII. - Good and evil typically befall those who possess an abundance of either.

XCIV. - The accent and character of one's native country reside in the mind and heart, just as they do on the tongue.

XCV. - The majority of men possess qualities that, like those of plants, are discovered by chance.

XCVI. - A virtuous woman is a hidden treasure; one who discovers her should refrain from boasting.

XCVII. - Most women do not weep over the loss of a lover to prove that they were loved, but to demonstrate their worthiness of being loved.

XCVIII. - Many virtuous women grow weary of the roles they play.

XCIX. - If we believe we love for the sake of love itself, we are greatly mistaken. (See Maxim 374.)

C. - The self-restraint we exert to maintain constancy is not much better than inconstancy.

CI. - There are individuals who avoid arousing our jealousy, but we should be cautious of being jealous of them.

CII. - Jealousy is always born with love but does not always perish with it. (See Maxim 361.)

CIII. - When we love excessively, it becomes difficult to discern when we are no longer loved.

CIV. - While we are well aware that we should not speak of our wives, we often forget that it is equally unwise to speak excessively about ourselves.

CV. - Chance reveals our true selves to both others and ourselves.

CVI. - It is rare to find people of good sense who do not share our own opinions.

CVII. - We often commend the good-heartedness of those who admire us.

CVIII. - Man blames himself solely to garner praise.

CIX. - Small minds are easily wounded by trivial matters.

CX. - Certain faults, when presented favorably, please more than perfection itself. (

CXI. - Our bitterness toward those who harm us is rooted in their belief that they are more clever than we are.

CXII. - We are always bored by those whom we bore.

CXIII. - The harm inflicted upon us by others is often lesser than the harm we inflict upon ourselves.

CXIV. - It is never more challenging to speak well than when we are ashamed to remain silent.

CXV. - Faults for which we have the courage to confess are always forgivable.

CXVI. - The greatest flaw of insight is not that it delves into the depth of a matter but that it exceeds its boundaries.

CXVII. - We provide advice but cannot bestow the wisdom to act upon it.

CXVIII. - As our merit declines, so does our taste.

CXIX. - Fortune reveals our vices and virtues, just as light illuminates objects

CXX. - Our actions resemble rhymed verse-ends that everyone interprets as they please.

CXXI. - There is nothing more natural or deceptive than believing that we are beloved.

CXXII. - We prefer seeing those whom we have benefited rather than those who have benefited us.

CXXIII. - It is more difficult to conceal our true opinions than to feign opinions we do not hold.

CXXIV. - Revived friendships require more attention than those that have never been broken.

CXXV. - A person who pleases nobody is much unhappier than one to whom no one is pleasing.

I. On Confidence

Sincerity and confidence may share some similarities, but they also have distinct differences.

Sincerity is an honest and open-hearted quality that reveals our true selves. It is driven by a love for truth, a dislike for deception, and a willingness to acknowledge and improve our faults through confession.

Confidence, on the other hand, imposes greater restrictions and demands more caution and discretion. It extends beyond ourselves since our interests often intertwine with those of others. Therefore, it requires delicacy to avoid exposing our friends while exposing ourselves, and to refrain from exploiting their kindness to enhance the value of what we offer.

Confidence is always well-received by those who receive it. It is a tribute to their merit, a trust we place in them, a commitment that establishes a bond between us, and a voluntary submission to a form of dependence. I do not intend to diminish the importance of confidence, which is essential for human interactions. My aim is simply to establish its boundaries and emphasize the need for sincerity and discretion, devoid of weakness or self-interest. It is challenging to strike the right balance between sharing our confidences with all our friends and being entrusted with theirs.

Often, we make confidants out of vanity, a desire to talk, and a wish to gain the confidence of others in return for sharing our secrets.

Some may confide in us without us having a reciprocal reason to confide in them. In such cases, we fulfill our obligation by keeping their secrets and entrusting them with minor confidences.

There are also those whom we trust, but they do not trust us in return. Yet, we choose to confide in them out of our own volition and affection.

With such individuals, we should hide nothing that concerns us and always present an honest portrayal of our virtues and vices, without exaggerating or diminishing either. We should adhere to the rule of avoiding half-hearted confidences. They only lead to discomfort for the giver and dissatisfaction for the receiver. They cast an uncertain light on the matters we wish to keep hidden, heightening curiosity and granting the recipients the right to seek more information and discuss what they have deduced. It is far better and more honest to reveal nothing than to remain silent after initiating a disclosure. There are other rules to be observed when entrusted with confidential matters. They all demand prudence and trustworthiness.

Everyone agrees that a secret should be kept confidential, but there is disagreement about the nature and significance of secrecy. We often contemplate what we should say and what we should withhold. Permanent secrets are rare, and the scruples against revealing them may not endure indefinitely.

With friends whose trustworthiness we are certain of, we enjoy a deep intimacy. They have always spoken candidly to us, and we should reciprocate in the same manner. They are familiar with our habits and connections and are perceptive enough to notice even the slightest change. They may have learned elsewhere what we have promised not to disclose. It is beyond our power to inform them of such information, even if it could be beneficial for them to know. We trust them as we trust ourselves, and we find ourselves in the difficult predicament of either losing their cherished friendship or betraying a secret. This undoubtedly tests our loyalty to the utmost, but an honest individual should not waver. In such situations, they should be prepared to sacrifice themselves for others. Their primary duty is to steadfastly uphold their entrusted secret. They must not only control and guard their words but also their casual conversations, ensuring that nothing in their discussions or demeanor directs others' curiosity towards that which they wish to conceal.

Often, we require strength and prudence to counter the demands of friends who seek to know everything about us and claim an unquestionable right to our confidence. We should never allow them to attain this unquestioned privilege. Certain incidents and circumstances may fall outside their purview, and if they complain, we should endure their grievances and politely excuse ourselves. However, if their demands persist unreasonably, we must prioritize our duty over their friendship and choose between two inevitable but contrasting evils: one reparable and the other irreparable.

II. On Differences in Character

While a great genius may possess all the qualities of mind, there are certain traits that are unique to them. Their vision is boundless, their actions consistent and active. They have the ability to perceive distant objects as if they were present, comprehending both the grandest and smallest matters. Their thoughts are elevated, broad, just, and intelligible. Nothing escapes their observation, and they often uncover truth even when it is obscured to others.

A lofty mind always thinks nobly. It effortlessly creates vivid, agreeable, and natural ideas, presenting them in the best possible light and adorning them appropriately. It takes into account the preferences of others and eliminates anything that is useless or unpleasant.

A clever, adaptable, and affable mind knows how to navigate and overcome difficulties. It bends easily to its desires, understanding the inclinations and temperaments of others, and advances its own interests by managing theirs.

A well-regulated mind sees things as they should be seen, appraising them at their true value, utilizing them to its advantage, and steadfastly adhering to its own opinions due to a full understanding of their strength and significance.

There is a distinction between a practical mind and a business-like mind. One can engage in business without personal gain. Some individuals are clever only in matters that do not concern them, while others excel in their own affairs but struggle with everything else.

It is possible to possess a serious disposition and yet converse pleasantly and cheerfully. This type of mind suits all individuals in all stages of life. Young people often possess a cheerful and satirical inclination, which can sometimes make them disagreeable due to a lack of seriousness.

There is no easier role than that of always being pleasant. The applause one may receive from criticizing others is not worth the risk of offending them when they are in a bad mood.

Satire is both the most enjoyable and the most dangerous of mental qualities. It pleases when it is refined, but excessive use of satire can make others apprehensive. Satire should be allowed when it is devoid of malice and when the person being satirized can join in the humor.

It is unfortunate to possess a satirical inclination without affecting pleasure or without a fondness for jesting. It requires great skill to maintain a satirical disposition without falling into either extreme.

Raillery is a form of humor that presents objects in an absurd light, while wit can possess varying degrees of gentleness or harshness.

There is a refined and flattering raillery that targets the faults individuals readily admit. It knows how to conceal praise under the guise of criticism, pretending to hide the good while actually showcasing it.

An acute mind and a cunning mind are quite different. The former is always pleasing, perceiving even the most subtle and imperceptible matters, while the latter never takes a straightforward path, seeking to achieve its goals through shortcuts and deceit. Such conduct is quickly discovered, leading to distrust and preventing true greatness.

A distinction exists between an ardent mind and a brilliant mind. A fiery spirit travels further and faster, while a brilliant mind is sparkling, captivating, and precise.

Gentleness of mind is an agreeable and accommodating demeanor that pleases when it is not insipid.

A mind focused on details devotes itself to managing and organizing even the smallest particulars. This quality is usually limited to minor matters but can coexist with greatness, elevating the mind above others when the two qualities are united.

The term Bel Esprit has been misused, as it encompasses all the qualities mentioned above. However, it is often employed to ridicule rather than praise, as it is attributed to countless mediocre poets and tiresome authors.

There are other epithets for the mind that convey similar meanings, but the distinction lies in the tone and manner of their delivery. Unfortunately, as tones and manner cannot be conveyed through writing, I will refrain from explaining differences that are difficult to express. Customarily, we say that someone has wit, much wit, or is a great wit. The variations in tone and manner make all the difference between phrases that may seem identical on paper but express different types of minds.

We can be foolish despite having much wit, and we need not be foolish even with very little wit.

To possess great intelligence is an ambiguous expression. It can refer to any category of mind or none in particular. It could imply talking sensibly while acting foolishly, or having a narrow mind that is suited to certain things but not others. One can possess a large measure of mind that is suited for nothing, and sometimes too much intelligence can be inconvenient. Nevertheless, this kind of mind can be pleasing in social settings.

While the gifts of the mind are limitless, I believe they can be classified as follows:

1.   Some are so beautiful that their beauty is evident and appreciated by everyone.

2.   Some are lovely but become tiresome.

3.   Some are admired by all, although the reasons for this admiration may be unknown.

4.   Some are so refined and delicate that only a few are capable of fully appreciating their beauty.

5.   Others may be imperfect, but they are skillfully produced, sustained, and managed with grace and wisdom, deserving of admiration.

III. On Taste

Some individuals possess more wit than taste, while others have more taste than wit. Vanity and caprice are more prevalent in matters of taste than in wit.

The word taste has multiple meanings, and it is easy to confuse them. There is a distinction between the taste that attracts us to certain objects and the taste that enables us to understand and discern the qualities by which we judge.

We may enjoy a comedy without possessing a sufficiently refined and discerning taste to critique it accurately. Certain tastes unconsciously lead us to particular objects, while others captivate us through their force or intensity.

Some people have bad taste in everything, while others have bad taste only in certain things but exhibit good taste in matters within their grasp. Some individuals possess peculiar tastes that they acknowledge as being flawed, yet they still adhere to them. Others have uncertain tastes and rely on chance to decide, leading to frequent changes and susceptibility to pleasure or weariness based on the judgments of their friends. Some individuals are perpetually biased, enslaved by their tastes, which they apply to everything. However, there are those who possess a clear understanding of what is good and are repelled by what is not. Their opinions are genuine and accurate, finding the basis for their taste in their intellect and comprehension.

Some people possess a kind of instinct (whose origin they are unaware of) that guides them in making correct judgments on all matters. They rely on their taste more than their intelligence because they do not allow their temperament and self-love to override their innate discernment. Their actions are harmonious, and their judgments are accurate, enabling them to assess the value of things correctly. However, in general, it is rare and nearly impossible to find the kind of good taste that can assign a proper value to individual objects while understanding their overall worth. Our knowledge is too limited, and the ability to form a correct judgment based on a correct assessment of good qualities is a rarity, particularly when it comes to matters that do not directly concern us.

Regarding ourselves, our taste lacks this crucial discernment. Preoccupations, troubles, and personal concerns present things to us in a different light. We do not perceive what relates to us and what does not with the same clarity. Our taste is influenced by our self-love and temperament, which provide us with new perspectives that we adapt to an infinite number of changes and uncertainties. Our taste is no longer truly our own; we lose control over it, and it changes without our consent. Consequently, the same objects appear to us in such varied aspects that we ultimately fail to recognize what we have seen and heard.

Section IV: On Society

When discussing society, I do not intend to address friendship, as they are distinct although interconnected. Society encompasses elements of greatness and humility, while the greatest virtue of friendship is to resemble society.

For now, let us focus on the particular kind of interaction that gentlemen should have with one another. It is unnecessary to emphasize the importance of society for individuals; everyone seeks it and finds it, but few know how to make it pleasant and enduring.

Typically, people seek their own pleasure and advantage at the expense of others. We naturally prefer ourselves to those with whom we intend to live, and they often sense this preference. This disruption and destruction of society arise from this inherent inclination. Therefore, we should find a way to conceal this love of selection, as it is deeply ingrained within us and beyond our power to eradicate. Instead, we should derive pleasure from the happiness of others, always seeking to please and never to harm their self-esteem.

The mind plays a significant role in fostering such harmonious social dynamics, but simply guiding it along different paths is not enough.

The agreement between minds alone would not sustain society for long if it were not governed and sustained by good sense, temperament, and the consideration that should exist among individuals living together.

Sometimes, individuals with contrasting temperaments and minds form bonds. They undoubtedly remain together for various reasons, but such alliances are unlikely to endure. While society can coexist between those who are inferior in birth or personal qualities, those who possess advantages should not abuse them. They should refrain from overtly positioning themselves as instructors to others. Instead, their conduct should demonstrate their own need for guidance and reason, accommodating the feelings and interests of others as much as possible.

To maintain a pleasant society, it is crucial for each individual to retain their freedom of action. A person should not feel obligated or dependent upon others, yet they should still derive amusement from social interactions. They should have the ability to disengage without disrupting the fabric of society. Passing by others or avoiding occasional awkward encounters should be within their power. It is important to recognize that one can feel bored even when they believe they lack the power to bore others. They should participate in what they believe to be the amusement of those with whom they wish to associate but should not bear the burden of constantly providing entertainment.

Complaisance is a vital aspect of society, but it should have its limits. It becomes a form of slavery when taken to the extreme. We should give our consent freely, and in following the opinions of our friends, they should believe that they are following their own inclinations.

We should readily forgive our friends for their inherent flaws, focusing on their positive qualities. We should often avoid revealing everything they have said or left unsaid. When necessary, we should help them recognize their faults, allowing them the opportunity to rectify them.

Politeness is necessary in the interactions among gentlemen. It enables them to understand playful banter and prevents the use of crude and unrefined expressions, which are often employed thoughtlessly when defending our opinions too vehemently.

The intercourse of gentlemen cannot exist without a certain level of trust. This trust should be mutual. Each individual should exhibit an appearance of sincerity and discretion that eliminates any fear of imprudent speech.

There should be a variety of wit. Those who possess only one type of wit cannot sustain interest for long unless they can traverse different paths and refrain from relying solely on their preferred talents. This adds to the pleasure of society and maintains the same harmony that different voices and instruments observe in music. While it is detrimental to the tranquility of society if many individuals have identical interests, it is equally necessary that their interests do not conflict.

We should anticipate what pleases our friends, find ways to be helpful and spare them annoyance. When we cannot avert misfortunes, we should empathize with them and gradually alleviate their burden instead of attempting to eliminate it abruptly. We should introduce pleasant or interesting subjects to replace the unpleasant ones, or at the very least, take an interest in their concerns. We should discuss topics that are relevant to them, but only to the extent they desire, being cautious about crossing boundaries. There exists a type of politeness, and we may say a similar type of compassion, that does not intrude too quickly into the depths of one's heart. It often provides us with the opportunity to understand everything our friends know while still allowing them the advantage of not fully grasping what lies within us.

Thus, the interaction between gentlemen cultivates familiarity and provides an infinite number of subjects to discuss freely.

Only a few individuals possess the tact and good judgment required to fully appreciate the essential aspects of maintaining society. We may desire to disengage at a certain point, to avoid becoming entangled in everything, and to shy away from knowing every kind of truth.

Just as we need to step back to view objects from a certain distance, we should also maintain a certain distance when observing society. Each perspective has its proper point of view from which it should be observed. It is wise not to scrutinize society too closely, for there are few individuals who allow themselves to be seen as they truly are in all matters.

Section V: On Conversation

The reason why so few people are agreeable in conversation is that each person is more concerned with expressing their own thoughts than listening to others. We become poor listeners when we are eager to speak.

Nevertheless, it is crucial to listen to those who speak. We should grant them the time they require and let them express even nonsensical ideas. Never contradict or interrupt them. Instead, we should try to understand their perspective and preferences, elucidate their meaning, praise anything worthy of praise, and make it evident that our praise stems from personal choice rather than mere agreement.

To please others, we should discuss subjects they enjoy and find interesting. We should avoid disputes over trivial matters, refrain from asking too many questions, and never give the impression that we consider ourselves better informed than they are.

Our conversations should be conducted in a more or less serious manner, and the choice of topics and depth of discussion should align with the temperament and understanding of the individuals with whom we converse. We should readily grant them the advantage of deciding without pressuring them to respond when they are not inclined to speak.

Having fulfilled the obligations of politeness in this manner, we can express our own opinions to our listeners whenever an opportunity arises, without appearing presumptuous or dogmatic. Above all, we should avoid constantly talking about ourselves and using ourselves as an example. Nothing is more tiresome than an individual who cites themselves in every circumstance.

We must carefully study the manner and capacity of those with whom we converse, in order to engage in their conversation when they possess greater knowledge than us, without undermining the wishes or interests of others.

Modestly employing the aforementioned methods, we can share our thoughts with them, making it seem as if we draw inspiration from their ideas if possible.

We should never express ourselves with an air of authority or demonstrate superiority of intellect. We should avoid convoluted or forced expressions, ensuring that our words do not surpass the significance of the subject matter.

While it is not wrong to maintain our opinions if they are reasonable, we should yield to reason whenever it appears, regardless of its origin. Reason alone should govern our opinions, and we should follow it without opposing the opinions of others or appearing ignorant of their perspectives.

It is perilous to always seek to lead the conversation and forcefully emphasize a strong argument once found. Politeness often conceals a portion of our understanding, and when confronted with an opinionated individual defending an unworthy stance, we spare them the embarrassment of conceding.

We are bound to displease others when we speak excessively and persistently on a single topic. When attempting to steer the conversation toward subjects we deem more enlightening than others, we should equally engage in any topic that appeals to others, stop where they wish, and avoid anything they do not agree with.

Not all types of conversation, no matter how witty, suit every intelligent individual. We should select subjects that align with their tastes and are appropriate for their circumstances, gender, and abilities. Furthermore, we should choose the appropriate timing for discussing such matters.

We should consider the place, the occasion, and the temperament of the person listening to us, as well as their state of mind. For just as there is art in speaking purposefully, there is an equal art in knowing when to remain silent. Silence can be eloquent, serving as a form of approval or disapproval, and it can also convey discretion and respect. In short, there is a tone, an aura, a manner that renders everything in conversation either agreeable or disagreeable, refined or vulgar.

However, few individuals possess the ability to master this art completely. Those who attempt to establish rules often end up breaking them, and the safest advice we can offer is to listen attentively, speak sparingly, and refrain from saying anything that may cause regret.

VI. Falsehood

Falsehood manifests itself in various ways. Some individuals are false because they constantly strive to project an image that is not true to who they really are. Others, despite having good intentions, are naturally prone to self-deception and fail to see themselves as they truly are. There are those who possess a genuine understanding but possess a distorted sense of taste, while others have a flawed understanding but exhibit some correctness in their taste. However, it is rare to find individuals who are completely devoid of falsehood in both their mind and taste. In general, almost everyone has some degree of falseness lurking within their thoughts or preferences.

This universal falseness stems from the fact that our qualities and tastes are often uncertain and confused. We do not perceive things with perfect clarity, and we tend to overvalue or undervalue them based on subjective judgment. We fail to align ourselves with things in a manner that befits their true worth and our own condition and qualities. This misalignment gives rise to numerous falsehoods in both our taste and our thinking. Our self-love is easily flattered by anything that presents itself to us as good.

However, there are many types of good that appeal to our vanity and temperament, and our affinity for them is often driven by custom or personal advantage. We follow the crowd without considering that what may be appropriate or uncomfortable for one person may not hold the same weight for others. We are more afraid of displaying falsehood in our taste than in our thoughts. True gentleness lies in impartially approving what deserves approval, following what deserves to be followed, and taking offense at nothing. But we should exercise great discernment and precision. We must distinguish between what is objectively good and what is good for us personally, and always follow our natural inclination toward things that please us, guided by reason.

If individuals sought only to excel through their own talents and by fulfilling their duties, there would be no falsehood in their taste or conduct. They would demonstrate their true selves, judge matters based on their own insights, and attract others through their reasoning abilities. Their views and sentiments would display discernment, their taste would be genuine and inherent, not borrowed from others, and their choices would be made deliberately rather than out of habit or chance. If we display falsehood in admiring what should not be admired, it is often due to envy when we assign value to qualities that are good in themselves but do not suit us. For example, a magistrate is false when he deludes himself into thinking he is courageous and that he would be brave in certain situations. He should remain resolute and unwavering when faced with a situation that demands suppression, without fear of being false, while it would be false and absurd for him to engage in a duel over such a matter.

A woman may have an affinity for science, but not all fields of science are suitable for her. Certain scientific doctrines do not complement her nature and are always false when she attempts to apply them.

Reason and good sense should determine the value of things, guide our taste, and bestow upon them the merit and importance that befits them. However, the majority of people are deceived in assessing the price and value of things, leading to these constant mistakes and falsehoods.

VII. Air and Manner

Each individual possesses a unique air that corresponds to their physical appearance and talents. We lose this natural air when we abandon it to adopt another.

It is important to identify the air that is inherent to us and never forsake it but rather refine it to the best of our ability. This is why children often charm others—they are immersed in the natural air and manner bestowed upon them by nature and are oblivious to any other. However, as they grow out of infancy, they become influenced by what they see and attempt to imitate it, albeit with imperfection and uncertainty. Their manner and opinions lack stability. Instead of truly being what they desire to appear, they seek to portray what they are not.

Everyone desires to be different and greater than they are. They aspire to assume an air that is distinct from their own, along with a mindset that deviates from their inherent nature. They adopt their style and manner haphazardly, conducting experiments upon themselves, without considering that what suits one person may not suit everyone. There is no universal standard for taste or manners, and imitating others does not lead to genuine copies.

Nevertheless, if individuals genuinely follow their natural inclinations, they can find harmony in many aspects without becoming mere replicas of one another. However, in general, individuals do not wholly embrace their natural tendencies. They have a propensity for imitation. Often, without realizing it, they imitate the same person, neglecting their own positive qualities for the attributes of others that do not necessarily suit them.

By saying this, I do not suggest that one should be so absorbed in themselves that they cannot follow examples or acquire useful habits that do not come naturally. Arts and sciences may be suitable for many who possess the capability. Good manners and politeness are appropriate for everyone. However, acquired qualities should always complement and harmonize with our natural qualities, subtly expanding and enhancing them. We are elevated to a rank and dignity beyond our innate selves. We often find ourselves in new professions for which nature has not prepared us. Each of these conditions carries its own air, but it does not always align with our natural manner. This change in fortune can alter our air and manners, intensifying a false sense of dignity that becomes evident when it is overly pronounced and disconnected from our inherent qualities. Therefore, we should strive to blend and unite these aspects, making them inseparable.

We should not adopt a single tone and manner when discussing all subjects. Just as we walk differently at the head of a regiment compared to strolling on a promenade, our style of speech should naturally vary when addressing different matters. However, it should always remain genuine and appropriate, whether leading a regiment or taking a leisurely walk. Some individuals not only abandon their natural air and manner to assume the characteristics of their attained rank and dignity but also prematurely adopt the air and manner they aspire to. How many lieutenant generals assume the airs of marshals of France? How many barristers fruitlessly imitate the style of the Chancellor? How many common citizens put on the airs of duchesses?

What is most vexing is that individuals often fail to align their air and manners with their appearance, or their style and words with their thoughts and sentiments. They lose sight of themselves and drift unknowingly away from the truth. Almost everyone succumbs to this fault in some way. Few possess the fine ear required to discern this particular cadence.

Many people with commendable qualities are displeasing, while others with fewer abilities are pleasing. The reason for this lies in the fact that the former wish to appear to be what they are not, while the latter are what they appear to be.

The advantages or disadvantages bestowed upon us by nature please us to the extent that we are aware of the air, style, manner, and sentiments that align with our circumstances and appearance. Conversely, they displease us when they deviate from this point of harmony.

*

Friedrich Nietzsche

1. Relentless desire always discovers means to ensnare life's inhabitants and compel them to endure, veiled by illusions cast over the world.

2. The pursuit of knowledge often stifles action, for action thrives when draped in the veil of illusion.

3. Existence and the world find eternal justification solely as aesthetic phenomena.

4. Tragedy, in its artistry, reshapes the dreadful or absurd aspects of existence into representations that humans can coexist with.

5. Facing existence, one must courageously walk a perilous path, knowing it's destined to slip away from our grasp.

6. We toil in our daily labor with excessive zeal, often thoughtlessly, not just to sustain life but, even more so, to avoid the leisure for contemplation. Haste is universal because everyone flees from introspection.

7. Morality did not conceive life; it thrives on deception and thrives through deception.

8. Observe the cattle grazing as they pass you by: they know nothing of yesterday or today. They live for the moment, free of melancholy or boredom. Man, in his superiority, envies their simple happiness, craving the life they have – untroubled, painless, and joyful. What he wants, he cannot have, as he refuses to live as an animal.

9. Remarkably, our scholars often overlook a fundamental question: What is the purpose and urgency behind their relentless endeavors?

10. Traditions become increasingly venerable with their distance from origin, as obscurity enshrouds their beginnings. Reverence for tradition grows with each generation, eventually sanctifying it and inspiring awe.

11. To escape boredom, man engages in work exceeding his basic needs or invents play, which is work designed to quell the need for labor.

12. Christianity emerged to uplift the spirit but now finds it necessary to burden the soul before offering solace. Thus, it may face its demise.

13. In truth, hope is among the gravest of evils, prolonging human suffering.

14. A few hours of mountain climbing can transform both a rogue and a saint into fairly similar beings.

15. Excessive admiration for a quality or art can deter one from pursuing it.

16. When suddenly asked for an opinion, our initial thoughts are often not our own but dictated by convention, status, or heritage. Our genuine opinions are usually buried deeper.

17. A man's character is more a reflection of his temperaments than his principles, revealed in his persistent adherence to either.

18. Where madness exists, a grain of genius and wisdom is often present. All great individuals who've defied conventional morality have had no choice but to either be mad or pretend to be, as they faced the difficulty of forging new principles.

19. Christianity has sought to eliminate all doubt, requiring belief without reason, through miracles, drowning reason in an eternal hymn over the waves.

20. Moderation often views itself as beautiful, but it fails to realize that in the eyes of the immoderate, it may appear dull and sober.

21. The surest way to corrupt a youth is to instruct them to prioritize conformity over diversity of thought.

22. Those in need of consolation find the idea that no consolation is possible to be the most effective, signifying a degree of distinction that allows them to regain their composure.

23. In the grand trajectory of life, one may reach a point where they can journey no further and settle in a humble place. Yet, do not mistakenly conclude that their vast and remarkable journey has reached its limit, for other birds will soar even higher.

24. I wish to develop an eye to appreciate the beauty in necessity, to make the world more beautiful, to embrace my fate. I shall not wage war against the ugly but seek to find meaning in it. My only negation will be to avert my gaze.

25. Living dangerously is the secret to the greatest productivity and enjoyment of life.

26. Seeking work solely for remuneration is the common practice in civilized societies. However, some refuse work without pleasure, as they find it essential that their labor is rewarding beyond the material compensation.

27. To withstand the unsettling ambiguities of existence without questioning and the longing to question is contemptible.

28. Living in a world of pretenses, superficial conventions, and play-acting for oneself and others is the norm. Authenticity is a rare and underappreciated quality.

29. Pity is most agreeable to those with little pride and limited prospects for great accomplishments.

30. Possessions often diminish when one possesses them.

31. The idea of 'God is dead' challenges the notion that supernatural beliefs are essential, raising the question of humanity's place without them.

32. While God may be considered dead, in the realm of human experience, remnants of these beliefs may endure, casting a shadow.

33. Emerging from severe adversity, one should find rebirth, with enhanced sensitivity, joy, and a desire for unique experiences.

34. The art of cultivating one's character requires a unique ability to meld strengths and weaknesses into a work of art.

35. Man is not the final stage but a transitional creature on the path toward greater possibilities.

36. Distrust those whose desire for retribution is potent.

37. The concept of God distorts humanity's perception of reality.

38. Minor inconveniences are often exaggerated as the worst of evils, yet more formidable challenges may loom in the distance.

39. In solitude, one's inner beast may grow. Therefore, solitude may not be advisable for many.

40. The Übermensch (Overman) would find the concept of the human being contemptible.

41. We vomit our grievances and call it news.

42. Creating freedom and saying 'No' to imposed duties demand the strength of a lion.

43. The Last Man, satisfied with small comforts, marks the end of an era in which humanity no longer strives for greatness.

44. Chaos within us paves the way to birth a dancing star.

45. Man is the bridge between animal and Übermensch, teetering over an abyss.

46. Individuals have their unique paths. There is no absolute right or correct way.

47. The Übermensch represents the essence of the Earth, and humans should remain true to the planet instead of seeking supra-terrestrial aspirations.

48. Whoever confronts monsters must take care not to become one. Gazing into the abyss, the abyss gazes back.

49. A person's maturity reflects their rediscovered childlike sense of seriousness in play.

50. Ultimately, we love our desires more than the objects we desire.

51. Contemplating suicide can offer solace, providing a way to endure difficult nights.

52. Independence is a privilege of the strong, as they face the labyrinth, while weakness fears it and stays trapped in the known.

53. Perception of the world often demands courage, as some truths are difficult to endure, unveiling the necessity for resilience, buffering, sweetening, and broadening.

54. That which does not kill a person makes them stronger.

55. Philosophers, often ahead of their time, have consistently found themselves in conflict with contemporary ideals. They become the conscience that questions the present.

56. Moral phenomena do not exist; there is only a moral interpretation of events.

57. Madness is a rarity in individuals but common in groups, parties, peoples, and epochs.

58. Memory often says, 'I did that,' while pride insists, 'I could not have done that,' remaining unyielding. In the end, memory concedes.

59. We must guard against the seduction of words, as our language shapes our understanding.

60. Despising oneself is a form of self-respect for those who bear disdain.

61. Sensuality can hasten love's growth to a point where the roots remain fragile and easily uprooted.

62. Christianity, with its teachings, poisoned Eros, leading it from vice to virtue.

63. Blessed are the forgetful, for they move past their errors with greater ease.

64. Love that arises from desire transcends the boundaries of good and evil.

65. Great philosophies have often been personal confessions of their authors, a manifestation of their unique and involuntary experiences.

66. One must either remain silent or speak with greatness regarding what is great.

67. Necessity is not an indisputable fact, but rather an interpretation.

68. Philosophy's role is to challenge prevailing perspectives and values, providing a fresh outlook to aid in the attainment of true objectivity.

69. The act of seeing is inherently subjective, as our perspectives shape our knowledge.

70. Man's inner world and 'soul' first develop through internalization.

71. Man's internalization of societal norms arises from weakness and results in what Nietzsche termed 'bad conscience.'

72. To demand strength to suppress its essence and manifest as something it is not is absurd, akin to requiring weakness to appear as strength.

73. Man, accustomed to pain and bold as an animal, embraces suffering when given meaning, for it grants a sense of purpose.

74. Man often chooses nothingness over non-action.

75. Instinct drives every creature to seek optimal conditions for their power, despising any hindrances in their path.

76. What doesn't destroy me makes me stronger.

77. The church sought to curb human passions through physical castration.

78. Reconnecting with our primal nature helps us heal from our artificial existence.

79. When stepped on, the worm curls up, reducing its chances of further harm. In moral terms: humility.

80. Idleness is the foundation of psychology. Is psychology, then, a vice?

81. Is man a mistake of God, or God a mistake of man?

82. Many great thoughts are born during a simple walk.

83. To develop a strong intellect, one must learn to observe calmly, delay judgment, and consider matters from various angles.

84. Freedom is the will to take responsibility for oneself.

85. Even the gods struggle in vain against boredom.

86. What is good enhances one's sense of power and will to power. What is bad arises from weakness. Happiness is found in power's growth, in overcoming resistance.

87. Great intellects are naturally skeptical.

88. The concept of sin was invented to hinder science, culture, and human elevation, to obstruct every advance and ennoblement of humanity.

89. To me, the world is an energetic monstrosity, boundless, enduring, marked by perpetual waves of forces. Humanity is the will to power – nothing else!

90. Art exists to save us from the truth.

91. When one encounters greatness, they must either stay silent or speak with greatness.

92. Necessity isn't a fixed fact but an interpretation.

93. Those who can inhale the air of my words realize it's rarified, born of great heights and unceasing light.

94. Resentment, arising from weakness, harms the weak more than anyone else.

95. Individuals should not be constrained to hide their strength and should not be expected to suppress their desire to conquer, to be triumphant, to overcome, and to have enemies and resistances.

96. Profoundly melancholic individuals often reveal their happiness with a strangling embrace, for they know it's fleeting and may soon escape them.

97. Self-hatred isn't a sign of humility.

98. Write books only if you dare to reveal the secrets you hide from the world.

99. I connect best with someone when they've hit rock bottom and have no strength left to maintain their illusions.

100. Profound and genuine truths are concealed, hidden beneath the surface of things.

101. Objectivity often reduces people to mere objects, treated with detachment.

102. If we could see ourselves as others do, we might question our existence.

103. Consciousness is not just a thorn in the flesh; it's a dagger.

104. Wisdom lies in embracing everything without being attached to anything.

105. We lose as much by being born as we do when we die.

106. Judging others is impossible; empathy is hindered by our inability to truly put ourselves in their shoes.

107. Most troubles stem from our initial impulses, and sometimes, enthusiasm can cost more than a crime.

108. Fear can counteract boredom, but it must be stronger to be effective.

109. Fear generates consciousness, which explains why animals don't possess a higher level of awareness.

110. The more gifted one is, the harder it is to progress spiritually. Talent can obstruct the inner life.

111. The nights we've truly lived are those when sleep eludes us, for restlessness defines a sleepless night.

112. No sensation is false; they're all real in their own way.

113. Like the madman Calvin, I believe we are predestined in our mother's womb and have lived our life before being born.

114. I feel free but know I am not.

115. We should have been excused from the burden of a body; the self alone is heavy enough.

116. Writing a book postpones a kind of self-destruction.

117. Death, a universal equalizer, gives us ownership of the universe without any effort on our part.

118. Mystics and saints don't need eyes; their hearts serve as their sight.

119. My Lord, without you, I am insane, and with you, I shall go mad!

120. Paganism explores the surface of existence, while saintliness delves into its depths.

121. Saints exist in the flames; wise men stand beside them.

122. Only paradise or the sea could make me abandon music.

123. To fear is to experience death constantly.

124. A heart without music is like beauty devoid of melancholy.

125. Could God be a fleeting invention of the soul, a transient passion in the annals of history?

126. Belief in philosophy keeps us healthy; it's our thoughts that lead to sickness.

127. Only light souls can be saved, for they won't weigh down the angels' wings.

128. We are the wounds inflicted by nature.

129. The collective wisdom of all philosophers can't match the wisdom of a single saint.

130. Sadness commences where creation begins, a realm where God has never set foot.

131. Music transcends all, with God reduced to an auditory hallucination.

132. A harmonious being can't believe in God; it's saints, criminals, and the destitute who make him accessible to the unhappy.

133. If truth weren't dull, science would have ousted God long ago, but God and the saints offer an escape from the mundane truth.

134. While humans are haunted by memories of paradise, angels are tormented by yearning for this world.

135. Saintliness is a heavenly vice.

136. Oppressed by the solitude of matter, God has shed oceans of tears, making the sea's allure undeniable.

137. Sadness makes us captives of God.

138. Without their madness, saints would be nothing more than Christians.

139. I wish my heart were an organ pipe to translate God's silences.

140. Tell me how you'd like to die, and I'll tell you who you are.

141. Man has evaded nature successfully, but this evasion is his tragedy.

142. As long as I live, I won't forget that I'll die; I await death to escape the thought.

143. From birth to death, each individual pays for the sin of not being God, leading to an ongoing religious crisis.

144. The yearning to hold God close, even as he slips away, leaves us cradling his lifeless form.

145. To exist is to be cornered.

146. Change your name after each life-altering experience.

147. Only a falling flower is complete, much like a civilization.

148. Doubt works like a disease or, more effectively, a faith, deep within.

149. A mute couple communicates through gestures, revealing the limited necessity of speech for happiness.

150. We cling to trivialities to avoid the truths they hide, deceiving nothingness with something equally empty.

151. Only the remarks of the ex-naïve, those who have transitioned to knowledge, interest me in a psychiatric work.

152. In sleepless hours, every moment brims with fullness and emptiness, vying with Time for supremacy.

153. Trying to cure someone of their deepest vice is to attack their very being.

154. Even as we advance, we drag along the indignity of being—or having been—human.

155. Friendship relies on conventions and compromises; it shatters when one partner exposes the other's flaws.

156. Eternity signifies absence.

157. Life is a vice—the greatest one.

158. When content with everything, we torment ourselves by imagining the sun's eventual explosion.

159. What to think of others? The mere existence of ourselves and others often seems strange and inexplicable.

160. Only that which remains unspoken and unexpressed exists and holds significance.

161. Thinking is a pursuit of insecurity; the thinker thrives on torment.

162. Death is often seen as life's ultimate goal, even if it defies logical explanation.

163. Fulfillment comes when we cease to be human.

164. Everyone is deceived, living in illusion. At best, we acknowledge a hierarchy of unrealities.

165. Old age is the penalty for having lived.

166. Hope is a form of delirium.

167. We find fulfillment when we cease to aspire to anything, becoming intoxicated with nothingness.

168. Life is abnormal; we are real only when we feel threatened.

169. We exist in the false until we start suffering, then we yearn for the false once more.

170. The only true dignity is found in exclusion.

Arthur Schopenhauer

1. A person can truly be themselves only when they are in solitude.

2. The final years of life resemble the conclusion of a masquerade, where masks are discarded.

3. In our monogamous culture, marriage often means relinquishing rights and doubling responsibilities.

4. Sinister thoughts and fruitless efforts gradually leave their mark on one's face, particularly in the eyes.

5. A face makes its most profound impression upon us during the initial encounter.

6. Mostly, it's through loss that we come to appreciate the value of things.

7. The spoken word endures longer than any material possession.

8. What people often attribute to fate is, in reality, a consequence of their own poor decisions.

9. It's the small, considerate gestures that distinguish us; fate may deal the cards, but we choose how to play them.

10. Scarcely anything substantial can be found anywhere in the world; it abounds with suffering and pain.

11. Isolation is the destiny of great minds, a fate sometimes lamented but ultimately chosen as the lesser of two evils.

12. A poet or philosopher should find no fault with their era if it allows them to work undisturbed in their own corner.

13. Writers who target a less discerning audience are assured of a sizable readership.

14. Life is given to us not for enjoyment but for overcoming, for getting through.

15. No one pens worthwhile words unless they write solely for the sake of their subject.

16. By nature, people are mostly indifferent to one another; in contrast, women tend to have more adversarial tendencies.

17. The majority of our sorrows spring from our interactions with others.

18. We frequently dwell on what we lack, rarely on what we possess.

19. In our attempts to fit in, we forfeit three-quarters of ourselves.

20. Life is a continuous process of fading away.

21. All truths go through three stages: first, they are ridiculed; second, they are vehemently opposed; finally, they are accepted as self-evident.

22. We can regard our life as a disturbing episode in the serene stillness of nothingness.

23. Politeness is to human nature what warmth is to wax.

24. Everyone perceives the world based on their personal perspective, as if it defines the limits of reality.

25. Thorns often exist without roses, but rarely do roses exist without thorns.

26. A person who does not cherish solitude will struggle to appreciate freedom; true freedom is found in moments of aloneness.

27. Sacrificing immediate pleasure to avoid future pain is a prudent gain.

28. Ordinary individuals contemplate how to spend their time, but those with talent contemplate how to make use of it.

29. Life is granted to us, not for enjoyment, but as an ongoing trial to endure.

30. The complexity lies in teaching the multitude that something can be both true and false simultaneously.

31. Satisfaction arises from freedom from pain, the positive essence of existence.

32. Happiness is found in the frequent repetition of pleasurable experiences.

33. Every possession and moment of happiness are merely loans, liable to be reclaimed at any time.

34. The safest way to avoid significant misery is to not anticipate great happiness.

35. Money symbolizes human happiness in an abstract form.

36. Wealth is akin to seawater: the more we consume, the thirstier we become. The same applies to fame.

37. Finding happiness within oneself is challenging, if not impossible to find elsewhere.

38. The chief adversaries of human happiness are pain and boredom.

39. The greatest folly is sacrificing health for any other form of happiness.

40. The happiest moment for a content person is the instant before falling asleep; the unhappiest moment for an unhappy person is waking up.

41. Religion is the culmination of the art of training and guiding human behavior; it instructs people on how to think.

42. Men are the mischievous inhabitants of the Earth, while animals are the souls tormented within them.

43. The eternal existence that resides in us is the same that resides within every animal; they are essentially identical.

44. Religions often veil their allegorical nature instead of openly acknowledging it.

45. A person cannot serve two masters; they must choose between reason and scripture.

46. To label the universe as God is not to elucidate it; it merely adds an unnecessary synonym to our vocabulary.

47. Religions are akin to fireflies; they require darkness to reveal their brilliance.

48. The philosophy of religion mainly consists of reflecting on commonly accepted assumptions that are rarely substantiated.

49. Religion is the metaphysical embodiment of the masses.

50. Pantheism is merely a polite form of atheism.

51. Religions are the offspring of ignorance and seldom outlast their source.

52. Nature demonstrates that heightened intelligence often comes with increased capacity for suffering.

53. The challenge lies in conveying to the masses that something can simultaneously be true and false.

54. The brain may be seen as a kind of parasite of the body, a dependent dweller.

55. After your death, you will return to the state you were in before your birth.

56. The less intelligent a person is, the less mysterious existence appears to them.

57. Sleep is the interest we pay on the debt of life.

58. To yearn for immortality is to desire the eternal perpetuation of a great error.

59. Life perpetually oscillates between pain and ennui.

60. If people were not so preoccupied with themselves, life would be insufferably dull.

61. The more enduring a person's fame, the longer it takes to attain.

62. Because people lack profound thoughts, they play cards and try to win each other's money. Fools!

63. A pessimist is an optimist who possesses all the facts.

64. I am frequently amazed by the cleverness, and occasionally by the foolishness, of my dog. I have similar experiences with humanity.

65. To determine your true opinion of someone, observe your initial reaction upon receiving a letter from them.

66. Conscience accompanies every action with the commentary: 'You should act differently.' Though its genuine meaning is: 'You could be different.'

67. Every nation mocks other nations, and each has its valid reasons.

68. Only a great heart is the principal qualification for action, while in work, a great intellect is essential.

69. Conscience accompanies every act with the comment: You should act differently, although its true sense is: You could be other than you are.

70. Every nation ridicules other nations, and all are right.

71. It is with trifles, and when he is off guard, that a man best reveals his character.

72. Great men are like eagles, and build their nest on some lofty solitude.

73. Conscience accompanies every act with the comment: You should act differently, although its true sense is: You could be other than you are.

74. Will minus intellect constitutes vulgarity.

75. To feel envy is human, to savor schadenfreude is devilish.

76. How shall a person be proud, when their conception is a crime, their birth a penalty, their life a labor, and death a necessity?

77. Rascals are always sociable, more's the pity!

78. The world is my idea.

79. Life is a constant process of dying.

80. Each day is a little life.

81. To live alone is the destiny of all great souls.

82. Truth is most beautiful undraped.

83. In action, a great heart is the chief qualification; in work, a great head.

84. Honor has not to be won; it must only not be lost.

85. A sense of humor is the only divine quality of humanity.

86. Time is that in which all things pass away.

87. Talent hits a target no one else can hit; Genius hits a target no one else can see.

88. That I could clamber to the frozen moon. And draw the ladder after me.

89. One should use common words to say uncommon things.

90. A high degree of intellect tends to make a person unsocial.

91. Reading is thinking with someone else's head instead of one's own.

92. Hope is the confusion of the desire for a thing with its probability.

93. Pride is the direct appreciation of oneself.

94. To overcome difficulties is to experience the full delight of existence.

95. Change alone is eternal, perpetual, immortal.

96. Hatred is an affair of the heart; contempt that of the head.

97. Treat a work of art like a prince: let it speak to you first.

98. Will power is to the mind like a strong blind man who carries on his shoulders a lame man who can see.

99. Music is the melody whose text is the world.

100. Any book that holds significance should be revisited immediately.

Socrates

1. A life left unexamined holds little worth.

2. Genuine wisdom resides in acknowledging your own ignorance.

3. My intelligence is in understanding that I know very little.

4. To embrace change, channel your energy into constructing the new, not battling the old.

5. One who cannot serve well will not master with excellence.

6. Discover your true self through independent thinking.

7. The ultimate path to honorable living is to genuinely be what we aspire to be.

8. The heaviest cost of refusing to lead is being ruled by someone less capable.

9. For humanity, a life without reflection lacks value.

10. True freedom emerges from the acquisition of knowledge.

11. The initial step toward wisdom is admitting your own lack of knowledge.

12. The harder you toil for a goal, the greater your elation upon reaching it.

13. There is but one virtue: knowledge, and one vice: ignorance.

14. Authentic wisdom dawns when we realize our limited understanding of life, ourselves, and the world.

15. The mind shapes everything; what you think, you become.

16. Be cautious when forming friendships, but once formed, nurture them steadfastly.

17. To exist is to act.

18. Cultivate the reputation you desire to have to build a good name.

19. The most significant mistake is living in constant fear of making one.

20. To change the world, commence by transforming yourself.

21. Education ignites a flame within, not merely fills a vessel.

22. The sole true evil is ignorance, and the sole true good is knowledge.

23. Wisdom commences with wonder.

24. The more I learn, the more I grasp how little I comprehend.

25. Beware the emptiness of a frenzied existence.

26. Strong minds contemplate ideas, average minds discuss events, feeble minds gossip about people.

27. To effect change, invest your energy in creating the new rather than opposing the old.

28. Know your own self.

29. An honest individual retains a childlike simplicity.

30. Achieving authenticity in a world bent on conformity is the greatest achievement.

31. Your only true possession is your own self.

32. An unexamined life lacks worth for a human being.

33. There is only one virtue: knowledge, and one vice: ignorance.

34. An education bought with money is inferior to none at all.

35. Wonder marks the start of wisdom.

36. The wealthiest are those content with the least, for contentment is nature's treasure.

37. I can't instruct anyone; I can only stimulate their thoughts.

38. To foster a good reputation, strive to be what you wish to appear.

39. An honest person retains a childlike simplicity.

40. The secret to happiness lies not in acquiring more but in appreciating less.

41. To influence the world, initiate change within yourself.

42. To sway others, first persuade yourself.

43. True wisdom lies in recognizing your own ignorance.

44. Genuine wisdom emerges when we acknowledge our limited understanding of life, ourselves, and the world.

45. Prefer knowledge over wealth, for the former is transient, while the latter is enduring.

46. Courage is having mastery over your fears.

47. The ultimate path to an honorable life is to embody the ideals we project.

48. I am not confined to Athens or Greece but am a global citizen.

49. The greatest blessings within humanity are both within us and within our grasp.

50. One who cannot serve well will not lead effectively.

51. When desire abandons reason and surrenders to pleasure's allure, it earns the title of love.

52. Worthless individuals live to indulge; those of substance indulge to live.

53. The highest glory in life isn't avoiding falls but rising each time we stumble.

54. A moral code rooted in relative emotions is an illusion, a shallow concept devoid of truth or substance.

55. The mind shapes reality; your thoughts define your being.

56. Invest your time in self-improvement through the wisdom found in others' writings.

57. One who cannot serve well will not master with excellence.

58. Discover your true self by thinking independently.

59. To bring about change, channel your energy into constructing the new, not battling the old.

60. The sole true failure is the failure to make an attempt.

*

Confucius

1. The determination to triumph, the aspiration for success, the drive to unleash your full potential – these are the keys that unlock the door to personal excellence.

2. Beauty exists in everything, but not everyone perceives it.

3. When it becomes evident that our goals are unattainable, we should not modify the goals but rather adjust our course of action.

4. Select a vocation that you are passionate about, and work will no longer feel like labor.

5. Our most significant achievement lies not in avoiding failure but in our ability to rise each time we stumble.

6. We acquire wisdom through three means: reflection, the noblest; imitation, the easiest; and experience, the most bitter.

7. No matter where you venture, do so with your whole heart.

8. Success hinges on prior preparation, for without it, failure is likely.

9. I grasp concepts through engagement: I hear, and I forget; I see, and I remember; I do, and I understand.

10. When I walk alongside two others, each one serves as my teacher. I emulate the strengths of one and correct the weaknesses of the other in myself.

11. True knowledge is comprehending both what you know and what you do not.

12. The strength of a nation is rooted in the integrity of its households.

13. The pace at which you advance is unimportant as long as you persist and never quit.

14. Wisdom, compassion, and courage are universally recognized as moral virtues.

15. Opening a book invariably results in gaining knowledge.

16. A flawless diamond is superior to a perfect pebble.

17. Plant a seed if you think in terms of a year; plant trees if you think in terms of ten years; educate the people if you think in terms of 100 years.

18. Expectations in life rely on diligence; a mechanic must sharpen his tools before perfecting his work.

19. A noble individual speaks modestly but acts magnificently.

20. Modesty serves as the solid foundation for all virtues.

21. The more a person meditates on positive thoughts, the brighter their world and the world at large will become.

22. Examine the past if you wish to shape the future.

23. Old age, believe me, is a good and pleasant thing. It is true you are gently shouldered off the stage, but then you are given such a comfortable front stall as a spectator.

24. I encourage you to be your authentic self, deep within your core.

25. Rather than fretting over a lack of an office, focus on how to prepare yourself for one. Instead of worrying about being unknown, strive to be worthy of recognition.

26. Never form friendships with individuals who are not morally superior to you.

27. The superior person is vexed by their own limitations, not by the lack of recognition for their abilities.

28. Use modesty when expressing yourself to ensure the validity of your words.

29. When you work for others, do so with the same dedication as if you were working for yourself.

30. Do not impose on others what you would not desire for yourself.

31. To be wronged is inconsequential unless you choose to remember it continually.

32. The superior person consistently contemplates virtue, while the common person seeks comfort.

33. I am unconcerned with others not recognizing me; I am concerned with my own inadequacy.

34. To possess knowledge is to admit what you know and acknowledge what you do not.

35. The shortcomings of a superior person are like the sun and the moon: they have their flaws, and everyone can see them; they change, and everyone looks up to them.

36. When we encounter virtuous individuals, we should aspire to match their qualities. When we meet those with contrary characteristics, we should introspect and improve ourselves.

37. The demand for ability continually outpaces its supply.

38. Virtue is never isolated; those who practice it will attract companions.

39. Set an example for others and engage wholeheartedly in their affairs.

40. Honor the book salesperson, for they introduce us to the books we need most but often neglect.

41. Life is genuinely simple, yet we persist in making it complex.

42. A regular person marvels at exceptional things, whereas a wise person marvels at the ordinary.

43. Without respect for others, there would be no distinction between humans and beasts.

44. When facing what is right, failing to act shows a lack of courage.

45. Confronting what is right and failing to act displays a lack of bravery.

46. A gem cannot be polished without friction, just as a person cannot mature without trials.

47. Silence is a loyal friend that never betrays.

48. Only the wisest and the least intelligent individuals never change.

49. Your life is a reflection of your thoughts.

50. Focusing on minor advantages obstructs the attainment of great accomplishments.

51. A stable, consistent character is near to virtue.

52. Forget injuries, but never forget kindness.

53. Human natures are similar; it's our habits that set us apart.

54. The superior person seeks within, while the common person seeks in others.

55. Those who seek to possess knowledge should act as if they never catch up to their goal, while also being wary of losing it.

56. Imagination is more valuable than knowledge.

57. Respect yourself, and others will respect you.

58. Learn as if you have not yet reached your objective, and proceed as if you are afraid of losing it.

59. All good things are challenging to achieve, while all bad things are easily obtained.

60. A fool scorns good advice, while a wise person takes it to heart.

61. To be truly content and joyful, relinquish preconceived notions of happiness and contentment.

62. Sincerity aligns us with the way of heaven.

63. Artful speech can distort the essence of virtue, just as minor impatience can derail grand plans.

64. Understand what you understand and acknowledge what you don't – that is the hallmark of a knowledgeable person.

65. One who demands much from themselves and little from others will avoid being resented.

66. Character serves as the foundation of our culture, while music represents its blossoming.

67. Sincerity is the path to heaven.

68. Strive to learn, as if you will never achieve your goal, and fear that you will lose it.

69. Fine words and an appealing appearance seldom equate to true virtue.

70. Hold your faithfulness and truth as your guides, maintain friends who resemble you, and do not hesitate to correct your faults.

71. A mistake left uncorrected remains a mistake.

72. Before you embark on a journey of revenge, dig two graves.

73. Combat the evil within yourself before condemning it in others.

74. It is not the failure of others to recognize your abilities that should concern you, but your failure to recognize theirs.

75. The wise person is unwavering, the benevolent person is without worries, and the courageous person is fearless.

Buddha

1. Don't linger in the past, don't daydream about the future; center your thoughts on the present moment.

2. The key to a healthy mind and body is not to grieve over the past or fret about the future; instead, live wisely and earnestly in the present moment.

3. Three things cannot remain concealed for long: the sun, the moon, and the truth.

4. Ultimately, these are the things of greatest significance: How deeply did you love? How fully did you live? How willingly did you let go?

5. On the path to truth, there are only two errors: not embarking on the journey and failing to begin.

6. Health is the most valuable gift, contentment the greatest treasure, and faithfulness the foundation of the best relationships.

7. Our thoughts mold us into what we think. When the mind is pure, joy follows like an everlasting shadow.

8. From a single candle, thousands of others can be lit, and the original's life remains undiminished. Happiness grows when shared.

9. If you genuinely loved yourself, you would never harm another.

10. Inner peace is the source of peace. Do not seek it externally.

11. There is nothing more destructive than the habit of doubt. Doubt divides people. It's a poison that dismantles friendships and severs pleasant connections. It's a thorn that irritates and wounds; it's a sword that kills.

12. Grasping onto anger is akin to clutching a hot coal with the intent to throw it at someone else; in the end, it is you who gets burned.

13. Regardless of how many sacred words you read or speak, they serve no purpose unless you act upon them.

14. No one can rescue us except ourselves. We must walk the path on our own.

15. Let us express gratitude and rise, for even when we don't learn much, at least we learn a little. And even when we don't learn a little, at least we don't fall ill. And if we do fall ill, at least we don't die. So, let us all be thankful.

16. To maintain good mental health is a responsibility; otherwise, you won't have a strong and clear mind.

17. To attain good health, bring genuine happiness to your family, and foster peace in the world, one must first discipline and govern their own mind. Mastery of the mind leads to enlightenment, and wisdom and virtue naturally follow.

18. The mind shapes our reality. What you think, you become.

19. Your life's purpose is to uncover your purpose and dedicate your heart and soul to it.

20. You can search the entire universe for someone more deserving of your love and affection than yourself, but you will never find such a person. You, like anyone else in the universe, deserve your love and affection.

21. Just as treasures are excavated from the earth, virtue emerges from good deeds, and wisdom emerges from a pure and peaceful mind. To navigate the labyrinth of human life, one requires the light of wisdom and the guidance of virtue.

22. When digging a well, water remains unseen until you reach it. Initially, you encounter only rocks and dirt to be removed. Once you've cleared enough, pure water will flow.

23. Be cautious in selecting your words, for others will hear them and be influenced, either for good or ill.

24. You only lose what you cling to.

25. Discover your life's work, and then devote yourself to it wholeheartedly.

26. We are the sum of our thoughts. With our thoughts, we shape the world.

27. The journey itself is more important than the destination.

28. Doubt everything, and find your own enlightenment.

29. The key to existence is to fear nothing. Do not worry about what the future holds; rely on no one. True freedom emerges when you reject all external dependencies.

30. Every morning is a new beginning. What you do today is what matters most.

31. Wisdom is not determined by how much one talks; it is truly determined by one's peaceful, loving, and fearless nature.

32. One peaceful word holds more value than a thousand hollow ones.

33. In a dispute, as soon as anger surfaces, the quest for truth ceases, and self-interest takes over.

34. Even death is not to be feared by those who have lived wisely.

35. There is nothing more destructive than passion, hatred, foolishness, and greed.

36. All wrongdoing arises from the mind. Transform the mind, and wrongdoing will wither away.

37. Purity or impurity stems from one's own actions. No one else can purify you.

38. You alone can save yourself. No one else can, and no one else may. You must navigate the path yourself.

39. True love originates from understanding.

40. Conquering oneself is a greater achievement than conquering others.

41. Anger will not be a source of punishment; rather, it is anger that punishes you.

42. Happiness is not found on a path; happiness is the path.

43. Compassion should encompass yourself; without self-compassion, it remains incomplete.

44. Pain is a certainty; suffering is a choice.

45. The night feels long to one who is awake; a mile feels long to one who is weary; life feels long to the ignorant who do not know the true path.

46. To comprehend everything is to forgive everything.

47. An idea that is put into action is more meaningful than one that remains as a mere concept.

48. When you recognize the perfection of everything, you will gaze at the sky and laugh.

49. Patience is the key. Remember: a jug fills drop by drop.

50. Share this triple truth with everyone: a generous heart, kind speech, and a life dedicated to service and compassion are the things that revitalize humanity.

51. Believe nothing, no matter where you read it or who says it, even if I have said it, unless it agrees with your reason and common sense.

52. A dog isn't deemed excellent because it barks well. A person isn't considered virtuous because they speak eloquently.

53. Show compassion to all beings, whether rich or poor; each endures their suffering. Some suffer greatly, while others suffer little.

54. Take charge of your own salvation. Rely on no one else.

55. Each individual is the author of their health or illness.

56. In the sky, there is no division between east and west; people invent divisions in their minds and then consider them to be real.

57. If we could see a single flower's miracle clearly, our entire life would change.

58. Ignorance is the darkest night.

59. I don't dwell on what has been achieved; I only focus on what remains to be done.

60. Happiness is elusive to those who don't appreciate what they already possess.

61. No external force can harm you as much as your unguarded thoughts.

62. People with strong opinions often trouble each other.

63. If something is worth doing, do it wholeheartedly.

64. It's easy to see others' flaws but hard to recognize our own.

65. If you don't care for others, who will care for you?

66. Hatred can never be conquered by hatred; only love can extinguish it.

67. A deed is not well done if it leads to regret, and if it brings tears, then it's unworthy.

68. The essence of well-spoken words is understanding.

69. Choose your words carefully, for people will hear them and be influenced, for better or worse.

70. Radiate boundless love to the entire world...

Printed in Great Britain
by Amazon

35697926R00051